'Next to the word of God, music deserves
the highest praise.
Whether you wish to comfort the sad,
to subdue frivolity, to encourage the despairing,
to humble the proud, to calm the passionate or
to appease those full of hate...'

(Martin Luther, 1483-1546)

WHAT PEOPLE ARE SAYING ABOUT THE BOOK...

"Wow, I wish I had this absolutely brilliant resource when I launched out as a Gospel artist many years ago! The solid information, helpful suggestions and practical advice contained in this book would have saved me a lot of mistakes…chapters nine to thirteen are filled with practical tips on song writing, making an album, marketing strategies and effective use of the various social media platforms."

Isabella Melodies, Gospel Artist

"Roy has charted the history of Gospel music in the UK and given every artist real tips and practical pointers to succeed with their music in this current climate. He really has left no stone upturned in revealing the cogs that make our industry go around and in demystifying the details."

Noel Robinson, Gospel Artist

"A fantastic read with a great balance of historical information and practical, current and relevant tips and pointers for both new and established creatives alike. Roy's wealth of experience certainly shines through in this book. A must read for Christian and gospel artists!"

O'Neil Dennis, Founder aStepFWD | faith in action

To the memory of: Bishop T.G. & Mother E. Francis

&

For: Kayla, Jelani, Hassani and Damani.

Stay in touch! Sign up to Roy's newsletter at:

www.rfproductions.co.uk/

www.instagram.com/royfrancisgospel/

HOW TO MAKE GOSPEL MUSIC WORK FOR YOU

A guide for Gospel Music Makers and Marketers

Roy N Francis

Published by
Filament Publishing Ltd
16 Croydon Road, Waddon, Croydon,
Surrey, CR0 4PA, United Kingdom
Telephone +44 (0)20 8688 2598
Fax +44 (0)20 7183 7186
info@filamentpublishing.com
www.filamentpublishing.com

The right of Roy N Francis 2019 to be identified as the author
of this work has been asserted by him in accordance with the
Designs and Copyright Act 1988.

ISBN 978-1-912635-44-3.

Printed by IngramSpark

CONTENTS

Introduction

The initial idea for writing this book came from Chris Day, my publisher, colleague, and friend. For a long time, Chris has been telling me to write a book and put down 'my extensive knowledge and experience of gospel music' so that others can draw from it. As I didn't see myself as a writer, (I still don't), I made all the usual excuses, but all this changed when I ran a series of gospel music workshops with Marcia Dixon at the Croydon Park Hotel in South London. What these workshops, ('Pathway to Gospel Music Success,') showed me, was that almost anyone today can record a CD and with the internet and social media, can have it available literally to the whole world with a few clicks of a mouse. But having the ability to record a CD is one thing, knowing how to succeed with the music is an altogether different matter. This is where *How to Make Gospel Music Work for You* comes in, for what I offer in the following pages is how gospel artists can do this.

How to Make Gospel Music Work for You is in two parts and can either be read as a whole, in two sections or as a reference book seeking out specific areas of interest. In the first part of the book I offer a personal view of how West Indian Christians came to Britain in the 50s and 60s as part of the Windrush Generation and how the music that they brought with them developed and became the gospel music we know today. In this section I also explain some of the reasons why they came, briefly sketch the economic, social and political background to them coming, chart the setting up of their churches and trace the development of their music. Like most West Indians, they never intended to stay anymore than five years but towards the end of the 1960s, their economic situation had improved and seeing what this meant to them and their children, they therefore began to rethink the idea of going back home and put this on hold for the time being. As Christians, this also meant looking for permanent places of worship. The network of Black Pentecostal churches that exists today in Britain is a result of this decision to stay and with their music firmly rooted in a West Indian church tradition, this is the legacy they've also handed down to us and to future generations.

In this part of the book, I also look at the music these early Christians came with, the music they played, the songs they sang and I offer a sneak preview of West Indian Church services to show what churches were like then. Other themes which I explore in this section are a brief history of gospel music, the British and American gospel artists who have influenced British gospel and what happened to the music when it came into contact with the songs of the Billy Graham Crusade and the music of Jim Reeves and Tennessee Ernie Ford.

To most people, the decade 1970-80 is considered the Golden Age of British gospel music and I show why, as well as chart the main achievements of the music during this period when gospel seemed to be everywhere in the country, on television, on the radio, in the news, in concerts, at church events, at charity shows, colleges and universities, and at major pop festivals including Glastonbury! During this time, every American gospel artist who was anybody came to Britain to perform and it seemed as if London had suddenly become the gospel capital of the world.

In the second part of this book the emphasis is more practical - a how to succeed in gospel music - and I offer a road map for gospel artists who are struggling with their music and show how they can succeed with it. Unlike artists signed to a record company, most UK gospel artists are independent and as such have to do everything themselves for their music. They have to find the finance to do the recording, the money to produce the CD, a Director to shoot the video, and on top of this, they have to acquire the skills to do their own marketing and promotions. Although there's plenty of information available to help them - much of which is free - they still need to know where to find it and crucially how to apply it to their music if they are to succeed with it.

In this section of the book, I offer workable solutions, tips, ideas and no-nonsense suggestions which some artists might find disagreeable and may even be put off by it. If this is you, I would encourage you to read through the book first, especially this section, as what you think you might need to succeed, with your music, might not be as hard as you think. Others of you will see this as a challenge and rise to it and you are the ones who are likely to succeed with your music, but you'll need a carefully thought out plan and action to do so.

For a clarification, I frequently use the term 'West Indies' or 'West Indian' throughout the first part of the book rather than 'Caribbean' which is the more politically correct term. I do this to distinguish between people from the former British colonies in the Caribbean and those whose colonial experience were with other European powers. I also use the term 'gospel music' ostensibly to refer to Black gospel music, as this is generally known, used and understood in the music business. I know the term today is very elastic, but I use it as how a musicologist understands it, as a separate and distinct genre of music with its roots embedded in the music of the 'Spirituals' and from which it has developed.

Finally, this book could never have been written without the help of many people who have supported, encouraged me, and significantly fed into my collective education and consciousness. For this, I'm thankful to all those who have played a part and I forever remain in your debt.

Roy Francis
October 2018.

Within three years, Nationalisation was a huge success. Output rose, export increased, and unemployment fell. Consumer goods rose also, especially among labour-saving devices like washing machines and vacuum cleaners with a corresponding increase in cars, radio and television sets. The construction industry saw a similar rise in productivity with thousands of office buildings constructed to provide work for the army of female workers coming on to the labour market for the first time. All in all the economy grew, and the country began to recover and prosper. Surprisingly in the General Election of 1953, Labour was unexpectedly defeated and the country returned the Conservative party back to power.

The Conservatives continued with Labour's economic policies and the economy continued to grow, bringing real benefits to many people. For the first time since the war, workers saw an increase in their wages and a rise in their standard of living. A real sense of economic well-being gripped the country, but it soon became apparent that in spite of all this economic success, there was an acute shortage of workers. The government's answer was to turn to its former colonies in the West Indies to try to help plug this gap. What the country needed were workers and as they were plentiful in the West Indies, what the government did was to pass legislation, 'The British Nationality Act', which conferred citizenship on anyone in the West Indies who was willing to travel to Britain to work.

At first the take up was slow, but as word got around in the West Indies that jobs were plentiful in Britain and that the country was crying out for workers, things soon began to change. The 492 West Indians who arrived at Tilbury on June the 22nd were the first to take advantage of this policy and it is against this background that the bulk of West Indians came to Britain in 1948, and in subsequent years in the 1960s.

"Large numbers of skilled, semi-skilled workers were recruited for hospitals services, while others gained employment in industry and transport. The 1961 census recorded 200,000 West Indians in Britain......of which half were Jamaicans."[2]

Most of the West Indians who came to Britain to work were agricultural labours who mainly farmed smallholdings in their countries. The majority were Jamaicans who were mostly in their thirties, and as they were young, they didn't mind travelling to Britain although most hadn't even visited Kingston, the capital city of Jamaica.

Apart from work, there are other reasons why West Indians came to Britain. Many former soldiers who had fought in the Second World War, and unable to find work when they got back home, were on their way back to Britain. Many also came to Britain to escape the poverty and poor living conditions in their homeland, while most Jamaicans came because of the effect of the hurricane of 1951 and also because of the restrictions that The McCarran-Walter Act of 1952 placed on them going to work in America.

When the first West Indians arrived in 1948, this was not the first time that Black people had been in the country as there is plenty of evidence to show that they were in Britain as far back as Roman times, during the Middle Ages and in the 17th and 18th century, when they were either slaves, servants, or the occasional 'free man'. Much nearer our time, during the first world war, Black people fought for both 'King and Country' and Black servicemen saw active service in East Africa, the Middle East and on the Western Front. In the Second World War, over 500,000 soldiers from the British Empire and Dominions fought for Britain including 10,000 from the West Indies.[3]

prayer meeting gives. A sermon in a prayer meeting was simply an exposition of a bible verse, a passage of scripture or bible story with the aim of showing each person how they should apply its meaning to both their natural and spiritual life.

After the sermon, the next stage is the 'altar call' which is an invitation to anyone who was not *'born again'*, (not saved, not a Christian) to have a chance to do so. A person would indicate this by raising their hand and they'd be prayed for. After this the meeting would end with the singing of a hymn, a final prayer and the 'doxology.' The 'doxology' which is hardly now ever heard, was once an integral part of West Indian Worship. It is roughly equivalent to the 'blessing' in an Anglican service, although in West Indian churches, the doxology was mainly sung but it could also be said.

"Praise God from whom all blessings flow, Praise Him all creatures here below, Praise Him above ye, heavenly host, praise Father, Son and Holy Ghost."[6]

At first Prayer Meetings worked well in West Indian communities and as their numbers grew, people began to add Sunday Services to these weekly meetings. These were mainly held in a pastor's house or in one of the senior members who had managed, by then, to buy a house. Sunday Services were more formal than prayer meetings and the pastor's front room was made to look like a small chapel. They'd be two rows of chairs on either side of the room, a small table at the front with a couple of chairs on either side for the pastor and senior members. On the small table there would be a vase of freshly cut flowers, a jug of water, two drinking glass, an offering plate, and a small bottle of olive oil would complete the setting. Why the olive oil? It was used to 'anoint' - rub a small spot on the forehead, when praying for the sick.

"Is anyone among you sick? Let him call for the elders of the church, and let them pray over him, anointing him with oil in the name of the Lord," (James 5:14)

Both Prayer Meetings and Sunday Services were every bit a West Indian Christian experience, and both were places where people went to worship, meet up, make friends, hear news from home and as a community, there would always be someone on hand to offer help, especially when dealing with officialdom. Many of today's Black Pentecostal churches started this way, including in 1952, The Church of God in Christ at 57 Navarino Road in Hackney E8, my father's own church in 1953 at 77 Berriman Road in North London and also in 1953, The New Testament Church of God in Wolverhampton.

The move to Church Halls

In the 1960s, both Prayer Meetings and Sunday Services quickly became popular in West Indian communities and soon there was a network of prayer meetings up and down the country. However, as these grew, it was soon obvious that the next step was to find halls to rent and once again, West Indians were faced with the same problems they encountered when first arrived looking for somewhere to live. At first, they made approaches to their local churches to rent their halls, but many refused fearing loss of respectability and even when they did manage to find somewhere to rent, many of these were dull and dreary places. Furthermore, in many of these halls before anyone could hold a church service, they would first have to clean out the hall from the previous night activities and then everyone would have to put up with the smell of stale alcohol and tobacco lingering throughout the service.

The Church of God in Christ - Britain's oldest Black Pentecostal church was one of the first to find a place in North London to rent, but it took a long time for others to find places to hold their services.

From the beginning, West Indian Christians placed great emphasis on evangelism, especially street evangelism and they would hold regular street services or 'open-air meetings' as they called them, both as an evangelistic tool, and also as a way of attracting new members to their churches. Open-air services were usually held on Saturday afternoons near to open-air markets where West Indians shopped. These 'services' were effective in attracting new members to the churches, and many people testified that it was at one of the open-air services that they first heard of the church they'd become a member of. This was one of the ways, these early churches were able to grow their membership.

In the 1960s, West Indians had a strong sense of community. Churches were places where on Sundays and at Prayer Meetings people would meet and as a community, every member knew each other, cared for each other, and looked after and out for each other. Even the pastor's role was more than just a preacher. He knew that even with a full-time job, his responsibility was to both the people within his church and to the wider community and saw it as his duty to visit anyone who was sick, needed care, support or assistance.

Apart from meeting the spiritual needs of his members, the pastor would also be involved in their welfare and it was this system of social care and spiritual support which helped the West Indian community when they first came to Britain in the 60s and is the soil in which the Black Pentecostal church first took root and from where it has grown.

West Indian Church Services

Once in rented halls, West Indian Christians found that they could worship more freely and as a consequence began to put down roots and started to grow as a church. Their services typically began with Sunday School, which in the early days meant the whole congregation as most churches didn't have enough children to separate into classes. A female member - one likely to be a teacher 'back home,'- would lead Sunday School. The highlight of Sunday School was always, 'reciting the golden text' or the memory verse, which everyone was expected to do at the end, and this always bought a great deal of laughter especially as the older members or those whose reading was not particularly good, struggled to remember what they had committed to memory.

Once Sunday School was finished, the next stage in the service usually begins with the singing of some lively choruses (up-tempo songs), which everyone would join in, sing and clap their hands. Choruses played a central part in West Indian services and although they are hardly heard now, it was once impossible to imagine a service without them. For many people this was the highlight of the service, a time when they could spiritually let go, without fear and inhibition, singing, swaying and stamping their feet in celebration and praise.

In the early days when churches didn't have any instruments to accompany their singing, - perhaps only a 'timbrel' (tambourine) - people would sing their choruses and clap their hands as if they were musical instruments. Joel Edwards in his book, *Let's Praise Him Again* describes choruses as songs that:

"incorporate a bold simplicity and urgency, conveyed by repetitive and uncompromising directness." [7]

West Indian pastors too were changed by these visits and as soon as they returned to Britain, many began to implement some of the changes they had seen in America. For example, some pastors restructured their churches along American lines, and terms like 'Diocese' 'Prelate' and 'First Lady' entered Caribbean church lexicon for the first time. Others started to wear clerical gowns and collars, something which was totally unheard of before these visits. A few even started to wear cassocks, crosses, and chains, again something inconceivable before these trips.

Although these visits to America were exciting, eye opening and life-changing, they weren't without controversy. One of the first things that surprised many of the young people who made these trips, was that although the leadership in their churches in Britain was Black, in America in the 'mother church,' the reverse was true, with an almost entirely white leadership and congregation. As a 'mother church' based in the American South, nobody had prepared them for what this meant politically and socially.

Secondly, having not quite got over this initial shock, the next jolt came when these young West Indians saw what American Christian women wore to church - jewellery, make-up, and to top it all, Black Americans Christian women straightened their hair! All these were routinely condemned and banned in West Indian churches in Britain as being sinful and ungodly, but in the 'mother church', they were openly on display. The contradiction was clear, as it was terrifyingly obvious but what was also interesting and deeply influential, was that although these women wore makeup and jewellery, they were no less spiritual, nor did what they wore seem to inhibit the flow of the Holy Spirit.

As soon as the young people got back to Britain, they began to challenge many of the inherent contradictions in what was permissible in the 'mother church', but not allowed in the churches in Britain. Many pastors, rather than sanctioning a relaxation of the rules or agreeing to fall in line with the 'mother church', tried to hold on to what was an untenable position. In all fairness, what they were trying to do was to hold on to what they themselves had been brought up to believe, but unwilling or unable to change, they precipitated an exodus - mainly women - from the church with many joining some of the new independent churches that began to spring up in London and in many of the big cities. Those who remained, simply ignored the church teaching on make-up and jewellery and chose instead not to be defined by what they wore.

Despite all this, many West Indian lives were changed by these visits to America and many young people came back to Britain determined to bring about changes in their own lives and in the life of their church. Many of today's Black Pentecostal church leaders in Britain are a product of this experience.

best-known number. Twenty years after they disbanded, Mike Rimmer reviewing the music in 'Cross Rhythm', described the track as 'a gospel number given a slightly shadows guitar feel,......a blend of pop-gospel and 60s beat music....with great vocals by Tony Massop.' Tony Massop was the original lead singer, but in 1969 he left and under his new name, Tony Tribe, made the first reggae recording of *Red, Red Wine* which influenced UB40's own hit version of the same song. [11]

In the 60s everyone on the West Indian church circuit wanted the Soul Seekers to come to their church and their fame spread far into Europe where they joined Rev. Ken McCarthy, (Britain's first gospel promoter), and played to large evangelistic audiences in Holland, Germany, Norway and Sweden. In Sweden they were very popular, usually making the national news every time they played there.

While the Soul Seekers were breaking the mould with their music in the 60s, there were other West Indian church groups branching out with their music also. Among these and others were The Singing Stewarts, Brother LaTouche as he was known, The Harmonisers and The Heavenly Persuaders.

The Singing Stewarts

The Singing Stewarts was an a cappella group that came from Trinidad. They were based in the Midlands and consisted of five brothers and three sisters. They sang Spirituals and West Indian folk songs and were active members of their Seventh Day Adventist (SDA) Church organisation. In the 60s they took part in a local BBC television documentary *The Colony* which was a regional programme that gave a voice to West Indians who had settled in the Midlands area. Their appearance in the programme brought them to the attention of a wider public and they received many invitations to perform including making appearances in Europe and at their International Church Convention in America. They were later invited to perform at the Edinburgh Festival in Scotland.

The Singing Stewarts recorded for a couple of independent labels, with *Here is a Song* - a mixture of spirituals - by far their most successful. However, by the mid-70s, their style of singing was on its way out being replaced by a new sound (gospel),coming in from America. Eventually, the group disbanded, and Frank Stewart, the mainstay and inspiration behind the group, after a series of false starts, emerged with his own radio show on BBC WM, *The Frank Stewart Gospel Hour*. The show ran for over eleven years, becoming one of the longest gospel shows on British Radio.

Frank died in 2012, and today he and the Singing Stewarts are remembered as pioneers of British West Indian church music with Frank both the inspiration and the person who almost single-handedly, broke the mould in getting gospel music played on BBC radio.

The Harmonisers

The Harmonisers were another of the early West Indian church groups. Brother LaTouche, a well-known banjo player and musician, started this group which included Icilda Cameron, Sam Grizzle, Crossdale, Winston Cumberbatch and Carmel Jones on bass. Carmel later went on to set up the Pentecostal Credit Union which celebrates its 40th Anniversary next year. Like most groups at that time, the Harmonisers played mainly at church services, rallies and conventions. They made a couple of records for a small independent label who only pressed enough copies for them to take around with them when they played but not as a commercial venture, as the West Indian Christian market was as yet 'undeveloped.'

In the 1960s music events like concerts didn't exist in the sense in which we understand them today. Virtually all music events were church based and as Christian record companies were in their infancy, they too didn't have any real influence on the music. Groups didn't do 'sets' either or had 'sound checks' or anything like that. What would happen when a group was invited to play at a church, was that they would turn up with their gear - instruments/amplifiers etc - set themselves up, usually alongside the existing musicians, and join in and play as part of the service. When they were asked to do their number - perhaps two or three songs - they would do so from where they were with perhaps the lead singer walking out to the front to sing. Once the group had finished playing their songs, they'd be expected to join back with the rest of the musicians and play to the end of the service.

The Persuaders

The Persuaders was a family group from East London which included brothers George, John, Noel and Hezi Dyer, along with their long-time English friend family, Alan Chadwick. They were well known in the West Indian Church scene and helped to pioneer the development of British West Indian church music along with the Soul Seekers, their main rival. As a group they came out of the Ministry Restoration Church in East London which was started by their mother, Rev Dorothy Dyer. Like most church groups at that time, they played mainly in the London area, at church services, rallies and conventions. Occasionally they made the odd appearances outside of London, including one trip to Belgium.

The Persuaders made one recording, *The End is Not Yet* and unlike other church groups, they played reggae. Playing reggae was very controversial as many West Indian Christians believed that this was playing 'the devil's music' but George Dyer, the elder brother and the mainstay of the group, remained firm in his belief that reggae is part of West Indian culture and that the church should celebrate and embrace it. On account of this, he stood firm in his belief and continued to give West Indian church songs a reggae feel whenever the group played, despite the criticisms he and the group received.

In the early 70s, John, the second eldest brother and bass player, left the group to join the Soul Seekers. Soon after the group disbanded and George went on to become a very successful and well-known businessman in the West Indian community especially in East London. In later years, he became a gospel promoter and was responsible for the success of Raymond & Co, fronted by his son Raymond. In 2015 George died, but he'll forever be remembered both for his pioneering work with the Persuaders, his work with Raymond & Co, and also for the contribution he made to gospel music. John, who left to join the Soul Seekers, now lives in Germany and is still playing, while Noel, one of the other brothers, is now the senior pastor of the family church in Walthamstow, East London.

Jim Reeves

Another person who significantly influenced West Indian church music in the 60s was neither Black nor West Indian, but it would be an injustice not to mention him. Jim Reeves was a White American international country singer who sang both secular and religious songs. He had many pop hits in the 50s and 60s, but it was his spiritual/gospel songs that attracted West Indians, whether they were religious or not, to his music. In fact, every West Indian home in Britain during the 60s and 70s had a Jim Reeves record, and even those who didn't go to church, would always play his music on Sundays. This was how extraordinary influential Jim Reeves' music was in West Indian circles.

We Thank Thee is perhaps Jim Reeve's best loved gospel album and of the 12 tracks on this album, half, *Never Grow Old, I'll Fly Away, I'd Rather Have Jesus Than Silver or Gold, Across the Bridge, Have Thine Own Way Lord, Where Do I Go From Here* and *This World is Not My Home* were all sang regularly in West Indian churches.

West Indians warmed to Jim Reeves' smooth, gentle, baritone voice and his song, *Where Do I Go From Here,* seemed to sum up what many felt; when in the early days when things were very hard and people didn't know what the future held, they would often sing and take comfort in the words of his song, *Where Do I Go From Here:*

"...lead me through the darkness and through each gloomy day. Take my hand, oh, precious Lord and help me on my way. Give me strength that I might find, abiding faith and peace of mine, and I won't ask where I go from here?" [12]

Tennessee Ernie Ford

Tennessee Ernie Ford, like Jim Reeves, was another American gospel singer whose music had an enormous influence on West Indian Church music, and whose songs were commonplace in West Indian Churches. Tennessee was a recording artist in the 1960s/70s who sang Country and 'Southern Gospel' songs. Unlike Jim Reeves, who had a soothing baritone voice, Tennessee's sound was more direct, and unlike Jim Reeves, whose gospel was slow and 'country', his songs appealed to West Indians because they were cheerful and had a mid-tempo beat which suited West Indian church singing as many of his songs could be turned in to choruses. Among these are:

When God Dips His Pen of Love in My Heart, I Can Tell You the Time, I Can Take You to the Place, Have a Little Talk with Jesus, Each Day I'll Do a Golden Deed, On the Jericho Road and *Precious Memories.*[13]

Unfortunately, today many of these songs are not heard anymore, but in the 60s and 70s, they were the staple diet of West Indian church music with many becoming choruses which is the highest accolade any song can have in a West Indian Church.

A Brief History of Gospel Music

One of the most significant change that took place in West Indian church music during the 1970s and 80s was the introduction of gospel music. How this came about is due to a number of reasons. Firstly, the children who had come to Britain with their parents in the 1950s and 60s, were making their own way musically in the churches by the 1970s. Secondly, this group of young people were also regular visitors to their 'mother churches' in America, and while there came into contact with gospel music and were influenced by it. Also, during the 1970s and 80s, gospel music itself was making waves internationally, and in Britain, it found a ready-made home in West Indian Churches, especially among its young people. To appreciate this, it's worth looking at some historical moments in the development of the music itself.

'The Spiritual'

The 'Spiritual' is the earliest form of gospel music. It originated in the Southern States of America and developed against the background of the Atlantic slave trade - the period from the 16-19th century, when Black people were forcibly taken from Africa and transported to America and the West Indies to work on the plantations that produced the cash crops (cotton, sugar, tobacco, coffee etc.) that made Britain and America the economic powerhouses they became. Once in the 'new world' on the plantations, slaves worked from dawn to dusk and endured unbelievable hardship and brutality with only the fittest and strongest able to survive. Mary Prince, a former slave in 1833, published an account of her life, showing what it was like being a slave.

"I have often wondered how English people can go out into the West Indies and act in such a beastly manner... when they go to the West Indies, they forget God and all feelings of shame; I think since they can see and do such things, they tie up people like hogs —moor them up like cattle, and they lick them, so as dogs, or cattle, or horses never were flogged."
(The History of Mary Prince - A West Indian Slave, 1831)

This type of brutality was typical and to easy the suffering and brutality of their daily lives, slaves would sing. They would sing as they worked, as they planted, picked the crops and later when they worked on the railroads. In fact, whenever and wherever slaves found themselves, they would sing. These 'work songs' as they become known, drew their inspiration from the Bible, especially the Old Testament which told of a time *'when God's people in bondage, would be free.'* Slaves would sing work songs to easy their burden and to fill their hearts with hope of a day that they too would be free. Slave owners encouraged slaves to sing as they worked, because they realised that the more the slaves sang, the better they worked, and the more productive they became.

For the plantation system to work smoothly, slaves had to be made to be obedient, submissive and above all prevented from escaping. To reinforce this, apart from the brutality of the system, slaves were compelled to attend church and there in the Master's Church, at the back or in the gallery, they would sit and watch in silence - away from the rest of the congregation - and hear that it was their duty to follow their master's instruction as it was the 'way of the Lord.'

"Servants, obey in all things your master according to the flesh, not with eyeservice, as men pleasers; but in singleness of heart, fearing God". Colossians 3 v 22

Slave masters often quoted this when administering punishment, cynically believing that this would make slaves accept their lot and deter them from rebelling and running away.

Slaves too ironically kept their own 'church', and although they weren't allowed to assemble as a group, they would often meet in secret, usually at some distance from the slave master's house and here at these 'campground meetings', they'd fuse the hymns that they had heard in church with their own music which they'd kept from Africa, and create a sound that laid the foundation of what today we today call the 'Spirituals,' - the precursor of gospel music.

Slaves were forever plotting to escape and whenever they could, they would rebel and resist and make plans to escape. They used 'work songs' to communicate their escape plans and to conceal them from their slave masters. In the West Indies, slaves too used 'work songs' similarly. They also used them to communicate among themselves and to mock their slave masters, who were largely unaware of their meaning. Christian slaves in America were thought to be the first to introduce 'work songs' as coded messages, and in the West Indies some of these seem to have come down through the ages as choruses, possibly echoing coded messages of a time long past. A couple examples of these possibly are:

*"Meet Me By the River, someday, meet me by the river not far away,
when my work on earth is done and my Lord shall call me home,
happy, happy home, beyond the sky, meet me by the river, someday."*

*"It Soon Be Done all my troubles and trials when we get home
other side. I'm going to shake my hands with the elders, tell all my
people 'good morning,' I'm going to sit down beside my Jesus; I'm
going to sit down and rest a little while."*

In America, *The Gospel Train (is coming)*, *Steal Away*, *Swing
Low, Sweet Chariot* and *Go Down Moses* are some of the best-
known Spirituals that contains coded messages of escape plans.
The message in *Go Down Moses* is that an escape is imminent,
in *The Gospel Train (is coming)*, the way is clear to escape, and
Steal Away operated on two levels. The first that the escape
planned could go-ahead *(Steal Away)* and on the second level,
that if a slave couldn't be free in this life, then they would
prefer to *'steal away to Jesus,'* meaning they would rather die.

In Britain today, *Swing Low, Sweet Chariot* is perhaps the best
known of all the Spirituals, mainly because English rugby fans
sing it at all the matches. The composer is unknown, but the
song is thought to have been written around 1865 by a former
slave, Wallis Willis, and became famous in 1906 when the Fisk
Jubilee Singers made a recording of it. The coded message in
Swing Low, Sweet Chariot is that it told slaves who had decided
to escape, what to do and where to run.

SWING LOW, SWEET CHARIOT

Words	Meanings	Coded Messages
Swing low:	*Come down here low:*	*There is a safe house*
Sweet chariot:	*Chariot from Heaven:*	*The 'Underground Railroad' (safe houses)*
Coming for to carry me home:	*Take me to heaven:*	*Freedom*
I looked over Jordan And what did I see:	*I looked in the Bible:*	*The Mississippi River*
A band of angels:	*Angels coming:*	*People on the Underground Railroad who helped slaves to escape.*
Coming after me:	*Die and go to heaven:*	*Escape to the North or Canada.*

Fisk Jubilee Singers

The Fisk Jubilee Singers were the first real exponents of The Spirituals or 'slave work songs.' They were a group of Black singers from Nashville Tennessee who were among the first students of Fisk Free Coloured School, which was formed in 1866 by the American Missionary Association to provide 'a liberal education for young men and women irrespective of colour' - in other words, slaves. In 1871, the school found itself in severe financial difficulties and at the risk of closing.

George Leonard White, the treasurer and music director, decided to form a group of singers, (four Black men and five Black women), and take them on the road to raise funds to save the school. White named the group after the school, but more importantly, he included in the name the word 'Jubilee', which in the Old Testament is a time when people who owed debts are set free to make a new start.

At first, the tour didn't go well as white audiences reacted lukewarmly to these singers who sang in an European classical style as well as, many people believed, the singers were getting 'above' themselves, wearing fine clothes and singing like white people. It was only when the group started singing the spirituals, the 'slave work songs,' that White American audiences began to warm to them and things began to change. White Americans seemed to enjoy the spirituals more than hearing the group sing in a European style and it was this change that helped the tour take off and become successful. With this change and their increased popularity, invitations for the group to perform began to pour in, including one in1872 from President Ulysses Grant to perform at the White House.

A year later, Fisk Jubilee Singers came to England performing in churches and concert halls. They were feted by the Duke and Duchess of Argyll, introduced to Lord Shaftesbury and sang for both William Gladstone, (the British Prime Minister), and for Queen Victoria. The Queen was so impressed with the group that she commissioned a painting of them which today hangs in the Jubilee Hall of Fisk University. A number of other tours followed, including singing in continental Europe, Australia, New Zealand, India, Hong Kong and Japan. By the time the group finished touring, they had raised enough money to pay off the school's debt with money left over to fund Fisk as a fully-fledged university.

American Black Music

All music goes through many changes over its lifetime and to understand how gospel music has developed from the 'Spirituals' to what it is today, it is necessary to understand the historical, social and political background to the music, as they are inextricably linked. In other words, the history of Black American Music is the history of Black America's continual struggle for freedom, justice and equality. Several landmark rulings have helped in this development including both the 1863 Emancipation Proclamation, and the 13th Amendment 1865. Both are historical milestones which resulted in free slaves leaving the South - the land of slavery and subjugation - to migrate to the North, in search of work, freedom, equality and a better life.

Once in the Northern States, these ex-slaves came into contact with a new religion that was sweeping the area. This new religion, 'Pentecostalism' began in the Holiness churches and quickly found fertile ground in Black communities. As a religion, it was new and very different from the one that slaves knew or were used to, and was also different to the ones that had developed in Black communities after slavery. For example, this new religion (Pentecostalism) didn't try to imitate European style of singing or worship, but expressed a freer and more culturally appropriate religious form. In the Holiness churches, people played drums, guitars, banjos, tambourines, they clapped their hands, stomped their feet, shouted, hollered and sang in a 'call and response' manner which every ex-slaves knew. Soon the Spirituals that the ex-slaves brought with them to the North began to adapt and change, as it came into contact with this new religion. It would, however, take the skill and influence of a few key people in the development of the music to propel it forward into the new age. One of the first to do this, was the American Methodist minister, singer, writer and composer, Charles A Tindley.

Charles A Tindley (1851-1933)

In America in the 1900s, the new form of music in the 'holiness' churches, (not yet 'gospel') came under the influence of Charles A Tindley. Tindley was a Methodist minister, composer and founder of one of the largest African American Methodist churches. He was born in 1851 in Maryland, a slave state, and although his father was a slave, his mother was free. Tindley's mother died when he was four and he was separated from his father at the age of five. Unable to read and write, Tindley taught himself to do so and by the time he was seventeen, he could read and write fluently. Like most Black Americans, Tindley's life began to change after the declaration of Emancipation and the ending of the American Civil War. He met and married Daisy Henry and, like many of his fellow Americans, looked North for the chance of a better life. Together Tindley and his new wife travelled to Philadelphia where he found work as a janitor at the Bainbridge Street Methodist Episcopal church. He worked there during the day and attended night school where he took a correspondence courses in Hebrew and Greek earning a doctorate in the process. In 1885 he was ordained and spent the next seventeen years as an itinerant preacher. In 1902, he was asked to become the minister at the Bainbridge Street church, the very same church he worked as a janitor when he first arrived in Philadelphia.

Tindley was an excellent preacher with a considerable reputation. He was also a great composer of Christian music and wrote hundreds of songs, many of which were influenced by the hymns that he knew. His songs were much freer and less inhibited than the 'Spirituals' and he would include musical instruments to accompany them, often interspersing his preaching with the songs that he had written. In 1916, he published, *New Songs of Paradise,* a collection of his songs which was very unusual for a Black church singer and composer at that time, and five years later, he had six songs in *'Gospel Pearls'*, an anthology of church songs, published especially for Black American churches.

Today, many of Tindley's songs are considered gospel 'greats' with *Nothing Between My Soul and the Saviour, By and By When the Morning Come* and *Leave it There, (Take Your Burden to the Lord)*, considered among his finest. *I'll Overcome Someday Day,* is another of Tindley's songs, which many people believed influenced the civil rights anthem, *We Shall Overcome*. His other great song, *Stand By Me When the Storms of Life Are Raging*, is thought to have influenced Ben E King's, *Stand By Me,* the latter becoming a big pop hit in the 1960s. It was given a new outing to great acclaim by The Kingdom Choir, at the Royal Wedding of Prince Harry and Meghan Markle in Windsor, in the UK, in 2018.

Unlike many Christian songwriters, Tindley's lyrics speaks both about body and soul, as he believed that a person's material well-being was equally important as their soul. He was able to show what he meant by this when during the Great Depression in the 1920s, he turned his church basement into a soup kitchen to help those in need.

Tindley cared about people and set up a number of initiatives to support members of his church and others in the wider community. For example, he set up a saving club to help people buy their homes, and took great interest in young people, encouraging them to be educated. He was also helpful in encouraging people to start their own businesses, and he actively took a stand on social and political issues when he thought it degraded Black people.

Today, Tindley is recognised as the grandfather of 'gospel music' and one of its greatest exponents. Before he died in 1933, he had established one of the largest African American Methodist churches in America with started with a congregation of 200 and rose to over 12,000 members by the time he died. As a tribute to him, the Bainbridge Street Methodist Episcopal church where he first worked and made his name, was renamed Tindley Temple.

Thomas Dorsey (1899-1993)

The next change that came with the music of the 'Spirituals', was the music of Thomas Dorsey. Dorsey is thought to have coined the phrase 'gospel music.' He was born in Georgia, where his father was a Baptist minister and his mother a church pianist. He learnt to play the piano when he was young and played many of Charles Tindley's songs. In the 1930s, Dorsey left Georgia for Chicago and while there became a blues singer, pianist and composer, playing for Ma Rainey - a famous blues singer. After experiencing a series of personal setbacks, along with harbouring a belief that God was calling him to use his talent in the church, Dorsey decided to turn his back on the blues and began to write and compose 'gospel' songs', becoming a member of the Pilgrim Baptist Church in Chicago, where he served as its Musical Director, a post he held for over 40 years.

Dorsey's style of gospel music combined African American church hymns with blues and Jazz influences. His gospel music aroused the wrath of the churches in Chicago and they refused to include his gospel songs in any of their services, criticising him for bringing the blues, i.e. 'devil's music' into the church. On many occasions, Dorsey said he was thrown out of 'some of the best churches in Chicago,' but believing this is what God wanted him to do, he continued to compose gospel songs, playing them and selling his sheet music.

At first, Dorsey found it hard in Chicago to get his music published by any of the leading music publishing houses and as a result, in 1932 set up his own publishing company *The Dorsey House of Music*, becoming the first Black independent publisher of gospel music in America. In the same year he wrote his most famous song, *Take My Hand, Precious Lord,* which many people know simply as *Precious Lord.*

Precious Lord is a song born out of tragedy, pain and loss, and represents a soul so weak, tired and worn, that its only hope is to rely on God to keep it from falling apart. As a song, *Precious Lord* was composed after Dorsey received news while away in St Louis, that his wife, Nellie who was in the final stage of pregnancy, had died whilst giving birth. And if this wasn't bad enough, although the baby she was carrying was born safely, it too died a few days later. Stricken with immense grief and pain, Dorsey in his own words said:

"I became very despondent and filled with grief. A few days later I visited my good friend, Professor Frye. We walked around the campus of Annie Malone's Poro College for a while, and then went into one of the music rooms. I sat down at a piano and began to improvise on the keyboard. Suddenly, I found myself playing a particular melody that I hadn't played before. As I played, I started to say, 'Blessed Lord, blessed Lord, blessed Lord.' My friend walked over to me and said, 'Why don't you make that Precious Lord?" [14]

Dorsey said he got a few 'amens' on that, and the words of *Precious Lord* began to formulate in his mind, eventually becoming perhaps the greatest gospel song that's ever been written.

Apart from helping to steer gospel music into the modern age, Dorsey is also credited with introducing the world to Mahalia Jackson, the greatest gospel singer and the music's first superstar. He first met Mahalia in Chicago in 1937, and they began to work together, with Dorsey writing gospel songs and Mahalia delivering them in her unique and inimitable style. Together they both helped to propel gospel music into the modern age and set it in a new and exciting direction.

Dorsey's influence on gospel music is colossal. He co-founded The National Gospel Choir Convention and during the Golden Age of Gospel Music (1940-50), his impact on the music was immense and his influence everywhere. Almost every gospel artist during this period recorded a Dorsey song, and his influence could be heard in the music of The Dixie Hummingbirds, The Soul Stirrers with Sam Cooke, The Sensational Nightingales, The Five Blind Boys of Mississippi, and in the music of Sister Rosetta Tharpe who toured Britain in the 1950s. Dorsey's music also influenced Clara Ward, Albertina Walker and the Caravans and much nearer our time, James Cleveland, Edwin Hawkins, Andrae Crouch, and even more recently, the Winans.

Dorsey wrote hundred of songs, 200 of which are gospel. His three most famous songs are, *It's a High Way to Heaven*, *Peace in the Valley* and *Precious Lord*, which was a favourite of Martin Luther King and was sung the night before he was assassinated. Mahalia Jackson sang *Precious Lord* at Dorsey's own funeral, and President Lyndon B Johnson requested it at his. Today, Dorsey's archive is housed at Fisk University in Nashville Tennessee. [15]

Mahalia Jackson (1911-1972)

Mahalia Jackson is perhaps the best gospel singer the world has ever known. She was born in New Orleans, Louisiana on October 26, 1911, and started singing in church when she was four. In her teens, Mahalia moved to Chicago and became a member of the Greater Salem Baptist Church. Although brought up a devout Christian, she admired Bessie Smith and Ma Rainey - two giants of the blues - but she never had any inclination to sing anything other than gospel music. In 1937, Mahalia was introduced to Thomas Dorsey, and she worked with him for fourteen years, accompanying him to gospel concerts, where she sang his songs, while he sold the sheet music.

An entrepreneur at heart, Mahalia realised that she wasn't going to make a living solely from gospel music and took a beauty course to provide an income for herself. After graduating, she opened a beauty salon in Chicago, working in the week and leaving the weekends to her music. Soon she began to attract a lot of attention in the churches in Chicago with her unique brand of gospel singing, and it was while working with Dorsey in 1937 that she came to the attention of Decca Records who signed her to the label. She achieved moderate success with them and from there went to Apollo Records which is where her music took off. She recorded her first big hit *Move on Up a Little Higher* with Apollo Records, helped by a white radio DJ, Studs Terkel, who repeatedly played the song alongside the rhythm and blues records he played on his radio show, helping to popularise it. *Move on Up a Little Higher* sold over eight million records, establishing Mahalia's reputation as a top recording artist.

"With her riveting contralto, Jackson was as captivating and popular as any blues singers, and with her gospel's bouncing beat, proved just as danceable, even to those who didn't go to church.'"[16]

With the success of *Move On Up a Little Higher*, concert tours and appearances came flooding in and Mahalia became so popular that she was given her own radio show. She made a few more recordings with Apollo - the most famous being *In the*

Upper Room, 'which further cemented her reputation. In 1954, Columbia Records came calling believing they could make Mahalia into a top International crossover artist. She signed to them and became a massive recording star. With increasing recording success, Mahalia was much in demand for concert tours, radio and television appearances. She performed on the Ed Sullivan show, appeared at the Carnegie Hall in New York City and was featured in the film, *Imitation of Life.* She toured Europe and was very popular in Norway and France, where she made a number of memorable appearance. Mahalia also appeared at the Newport Jazz festival to great acclaim and worked with a number of legendary secular artists including Louis Armstrong and Duke Ellington. Mahalia was the first artist to popularise gospel music globally and became its first superstar.

During her lifetime, Mahalia turned down many offers to sing secular music, refusing to sing any songs other than religious ones. Also, she wouldn't sing in 'surroundings' that she considered inappropriate as an example of her unshakeable faith in God and gospel music. Apart from her music, Mahalia was active in the Civil Rights Movement and became a great friend of Dr Martin Luther King. In 1963, she sang at the well-known 'March on Washington' demonstration, where King made his famous, 'I Have a Dream' speech and was invited to sing at the Inauguration of President John F Kennedy. In 1968, she sang *Precious Lord* at Dr Martin Luther King's funeral and ironically, when she died in 1972, a young Aretha Franklin sang *Precious Lord* at her funeral, as if the baton of gospel music had been passed on from one generation to the next.

The American Influence on British Gospel Music

Many American gospel artists have influenced British gospel music but by far the four most important are: Edwin Hawkins, James Cleveland, Andrae Crouch and The Winans. Edwin Hawkins, because of *Oh Happy Day*, James Cleveland, due to his enormous influence on gospel choir music, Andrae Crouch, because he was the first genuine international gospel artist of the modern age, and The Winans because of their influence on urban gospel, and also because they were the first gospel pin-up boys of the modern age.

Edwin Hawkins (1943-2018)

Edwin Hawkins, the first of these 'gospel greats', burst onto the international music scene in 1969 with a re-working of an old church hymn, *Oh Happy Day that Fixed my Choice*. Most West Indian churches knew this song when it was released as it was always sung at Baptismal Services and at 'Altar Calls'. What Edwin did, was to rework this old hymn, write a new arrangement to it, give it a modern beat and in the process, created a phenomenon. When *Oh, Happy Day* was released in 1969, it became a massive international hit and went on to top the pop charts around the world. It reached No 4 in America,

Number 2 in the UK and Number 1 in France and Germany. It sold over seven million copies when it was released, and as the song was out of copyright, Edwin was able to claim all the rights to it as well as the revenue.

What *Oh Happy Day* showed, was that the music that began on the plantations of the American south was now a global phenomenon. It was on *Top of the Pops* in Britain, on the radio, on television, in the news, in magazines, and in newspapers all over the world. On the back of this success Edwin toured Britain, playing to sell-out concerts in halls and venues once reserved only for big pop acts. *Oh, Happy Day* was so influential, that in the 1980s, a number of British record companies thought the next big music was going to be gospel and went out to Black Pentecostal churches, looking for gospel choirs who could replicate what Edwin had done fifteen years earlier! It's no coincidence that both The London Community Gospel Choir and The Inspirational Choir were signed to major record labels then.

As a song, *Oh, Happy Day* was hugely influential and has been recorded by the good and great. Elvis Presley recorded it, as did Aretha Franklin, The Four Seasons, Glen Campbell, Johnny Mathis and Lady Smith Mambazo. George Harrison, counts it as the inspiration behind his own, huge hit, *My Sweet Lord.*

Today 40 years later, *Oh Happy Day* is still very popular with British audiences and gospel choirs are continually being asked to sing it whenever they perform. It is as if *Oh Happy Day* is indelibly printed on the mind of the great British public, as the song they associate with gospel music.

James Cleveland (1931-1991)

James Cleveland is a monumental figure in gospel music and one of its most significant artists. He is perhaps the most influential since Thomas Dorsey and Mahalia Jackson, and his name will forever be synonymous with gospel choirs, and the gospel choral sound that he, more than any other, helped to create. He was born in Chicago in 1931 and as a boy began singing at the Pilgrim Baptist Church where Thomas Dorsey was the Music Director. Over the years, Mahalia Jackson, Aretha Franklin and Edwin Hawkins came to sing at the Pilgrim Baptist Church and during the Civil Rights era, Martin Luther King preached there frequently.

Under the guidance of Dorsey, Cleveland learnt how to sing and play the piano, and during his formative years he came under the influence of Roberta Martin, a gospel pioneer and a Thomas Dorsey devotee. It was while working with the Roberta Martin Singers that Cleveland developed his singing and playing style and took his first steps at composing. In 1952 he joined the legendary Caravans led by Albertina Walker, which featured a young Shirley Caesar and it was while singing with them that Cleveland came to prominence, singing on many of their earliest recordings.

In 1962 as a recognised artist in his own right, Cleveland signed to Savoy Records and recorded over 100 albums with them. *Peace Be Still* is his most famous and when it was released, sold over a million copies and stayed in the gospel charts for over 15 years. The 1960s was Cleveland's most productive period and during that time he became the best paid American gospel artist and guided the careers of Aretha Franklin and Billy Preston, who both went on to achieve international fame in the secular world. Cleveland chose however to remain in gospel music.

After a spell as Minister of Music at Grace Memorial Church of God in Christ in Los Angeles, Cleveland left to pastor his own church, The Cornerstone Institutional Baptist Church. He formed two iconic gospel choirs, The Angelic Choir and the Southern California Community Choir, both of which he used to express his distinctive and original style of gospel choir music and directing. In 1967, he set up The Gospel Music Workshop of America, (GMWA), where he taught singing, directing, harmony, organ and piano as well as initiating workshops on the business side of gospel music.

Today, the GMWA has over 150 chapters, 300,000 members and is credited with giving gospel artists like John P. Kee, Kirk Franklin and Yolanda Adams their first big break. In 1972, Cleveland recorded *Amazing Grace* for Atlantic Records which featured Aretha Franklin and his own Southern California Community Choir. This is one of the most celebrated gospel recording of the modern age and when it was released on June 1st 1972, it went on to win a Grammy and became one of the biggest selling gospel albums of all time.

British gospel choirs are big fans of James Cleveland and his music and during the 1970s and 80s, most British gospel choirs patterned their music and style of choir singing on Cleveland's choirs and routinely sang his songs. In the 80s, he came to Britain for a series of television shows including a Granada ITV Special. This was the moment Cleveland's army of Britain gospel fans was waiting for to get a chance to see the great man and his world-famous choir. Unfortunately, he didn't have the opportunity to work directly with any British gospel choirs, but that didn't diminish his influence or the effect he had on British gospel music.

Today Cleveland's enduring legacy are his recordings, the two iconic gospel choirs he formed and the distinctive gospel choir sound that he created. He is one of gospel music's 'greats,' having won five Grammys, the last posthumously in 1999. In 1981, was awarded a Star on the Hollywood Walk of Fame, the first gospel artist to do so.[17]

Andraé Crouch (1942-2015)

Modern-day gospel music owes a lot to Andraé Crouch and he, perhaps more than any other modern gospel artist, has had the most enduring and lasting influence on present-day gospel music. He is an all-time great, and when in 1966 he introduced his style of gospel music - a mixture of traditional gospel, fused with elements of pop, soul, R&B and jazz funk - it was revolutionary. Andraé's gospel was music for a modern age - a music that appealed to both Black and white audiences and yet was deeply rooted in a Black gospel music tradition. As an accomplished artist, musician and songwriter, Andraé wrote beautiful songs with some wonderful melodies. His lyrics were also very different from his contemporaries as it emphasised the love and mercy of God, rather than sin, hell and damnation, so much a feature of the Holiness and Pentecostal churches of his generation. Andraé's gospel music is all about an enjoyable Christianity rather than one that concentrates on 'thou shalt not', and all his songs reflects this theme. Examples of these are:

Take Me Back, Soon and Very Soon, The Blood Will Never Lose its Power, Through it All, Oh It Is Jesus and *I Don't Know Why Jesus Loves Me.*

Throughout his life, Andraé was influential both inside and outside of gospel music. He was a recognised singer, writer, arranger and producer, and during his lifetime worked with many of the biggest names in the pop music business. He worked with Paul Simon, Quincy Jones, Julio Iglesias, Elton John, Stevie Wonder and Diana Ross. He worked with Michael Jackson on *Man in the Mirror*, Madonna on *Like A Prayer* and on three films, *The Colour Purple*, Disney's *The Lion King* and *Once Upon a Forest*. In the late 80s and early 90s, he was a frequent visitor to Britain coming to do concerts and television performances. His last television appearance in Britain was in 1999 on a BBC *Songs of Praise* programme, which I produced. Sadly, Andraé died in 2015, but he will always be remembered as one of the greatest gospel artist, singer, songwriter and producer whose influence on gospel music is incalculable.

The Winans

The Winans were Andraé Crouch's protégés and when they burst onto the gospel music scene in 1983, they were sensational. The Winans helped to popularise a new form of gospel music - Urban Gospel - which sent gospel music off in a new and exciting direction. Marvin, Calvin, Ronald and Michael were the pin-up boys of gospel music in the 80s and when they came to London for two sell-out concerts, their impact was immediate. British gospel fans took to them instantly. Here was a male gospel group, not a choir, who were slick, stylish and good-looking. They were also modern, could sing, had gospel and R & B appeal, and yet were every bit Black Pentecostal church! British gospel fans loved them, every gospel group in the country suddenly wanted to be like The Winans, and every female fan, had their 'favourite' Winans!

In 1981 they released their first gospel album, *Introducing the Winans* which Andraé Crouch produced. A series of other albums followed, featuring some classic Winans songs; *The Question Is, Restoration, Long Time Comin'* and *Tomorrow.*

With this success, the group joined Quincy Jones's Qwest record label and there they continued to produce gospel hits including, *Let My People Go, Decision, Count it All Joy*, and their first crossover hit, *Ain't No Need to Worry* featuring Anita Baker. This album, with its broader commercial appeal, won three Grammys and brought in a new young secular audience to the music. The Winans were the biggest gospel group in the 80s and were the first group to make gospel music 'cool'!

The Golden Age of British Gospel Music

The term 'golden age' is often an over-used term which is normally associated with high levels of activity and achievement in music and the arts. The 1980s is considered the 'golden age' of British Gospel music, for it was a time when much was happening with the music in the country. Then, gospel choirs, groups and singers seemed to be everywhere. They were on television, on the radio, in concerts, at church events, at charity shows, colleges and universities, and at major pop festivals including Glastonbury!

During the decade also a record number of gospel acts were signed to major record companies. They included The London Community Gospel Choir, The Inspirational Choir, Paul Johnson, Nu Colours, the late Lavine Hudson, the Doyley Brothers, and later in the decade, The Escoffery Sisters. Although not signed, The Angelic Voice Choir, Trumpets of Zion, Brian Powell, The Spirit of Watts, The Wade Brothers, The Wood Green Gospel Choir, Highgate Choir and The Merry Bells Choir, although not signed, were all 'big' names on the British gospel music scene.

During this decade also, American Gospel artists were frequent visitors to the country and the list of those who came to perform, reads like a 'who's who' in gospel music. They included The Clark Sisters, who as part of The Church of God in Christ were one of the first. The Winans came, so did Milton Brunston and the Thompson Community Choir. Andraé and Sandra Crouch came, as did Shirley Caesar, Donnie Harper and the New Jersey Mass Choir, The Mighty Clouds of Joy, The Five Blind Boys of Alabama, Phil and Brenda Nicholas, Richard Smallwood, Tramaine Hawkins, Yolanda Adams, Commission, Bobby Jones, Helen Baylor, the William Brothers and the late great Thomas Whitfield. It seemed as if London had suddenly become the gospel music capital of the world.

Gospel was even in the West End during this period and the sound track to the music could be heard in the productions of *Amen Corner*, the famous play by James Baldwin, in *King*, the musical based on the life of the great man and in *Mama I Want to Sing*, a musical which charted the life of the soul singer, Doris Troy, from her humble upbringing in the church to the West End stage.

Radio

Gospel music was also on radio both directly and indirectly during the 80s. Apart from hearing it directly, if you listened carefully, you could hear its influence in the music of James Brown, Aretha Franklin, Stevie Wonder, The Supremes, The Temptations, Marvin Gaye, Smokey Robinson, Al Green, Curtis Mayfield, The Staple Singers and virtually every Motown artist. What's more, in the interviews these artists gave, they would frequently mention their church and gospel upbringing, adding to the sense of gospel music being everywhere.

Gospel music was also on mainstream radio in Britain during the 'golden decade.' Gary Byrd was on Radio 1 with his *Sweet Inspiration* gospel show, Al Matthews was on Capital FM and Dave 'P' had his own *Gospel Show* on Choice FM. Brother Michael Francis (no relation) was on the radio in North London and outside the capital, gospel music was also on the airwaves at BBC Radio Leicester with Dulcie Dixon, with John McPherson at Radio Sheffield and the late Frank Stewart was at BBC Radio WM in Birmingham. Generally, the feeling in the country was that Gospel music was everywhere, out of the church and on to the world stage.

Both the Inspirational Choir and The London Community Gospel Choir came to the fore during this time and were frequently on the radio, in concerts, in the press and on television. These two choirs were the trail blazers in the 80s, taking gospel music out of the church and into 'the byways and hedges,' and although they were criticised in some quarters for doing this, they spearheaded the music that began in West Indian churches and blossomed out into society and out to secular audiences. Not everyone was happy with the direction the music was taking but this was nothing new, as the history of gospel music is littered with this kind of reaction, especially when the music seeks to go in a new and decisive direction. However, those at the forefront of this change took comfort that if Thomas Dorsey, the father of gospel music, could be thrown out of 'some of the best churches' in America for playing gospel music, they knew they were in good company.

The London Community Gospel Choir (LCGC)

The London Gospel Community Choir was started by Bazil Meade, Lawrence Johnson, Delroy Powell, and my brother, John Francis. The original idea was for a gospel community

shops! And if to add insult to injury, it was Christmas and all the pressing plants were closed for the holidays with no hope of opening before the New Year! When this came, although CBS tried to rescue the situation, the momentum was lost, and as a result, *Abide With Me* only reached number 36 in the national charts when it was a potential top 10 at least! [18]

Not everyone agreed with the direction CBS took with the Inspirational choir's album, and *Sweet Inspiration* received mixed reviews when it was released. The main criticism was that the album was a 'middle of the road' album and although its general thrust was traditional gospel, the lush strings and choral arrangements on some of the tracks were not to everyone's liking. Some people were also critical because they believed the choir's traditional gospel sound, which it had built its name and reputation on, was compromised.

Whatever the rights or wrongs of the direction CBS took with the album, the choir signed to them was a major achievement, as it opened doors both for the choir and for British gospel music. It also gave John a platform from which to start his ministry, and although the choir is long disbanded and no more, echoes of them can still be heard at Ruach City Community Church where John is the senior pastor. It's all a far cry from a very humble beginning that all started in a small church at, 71 White Lion Street in Islington, North London.

Apart from the London Community Gospel Choir and The Inspirational Choir, there were other gospel acts who in their separate and collective way, were all blazing the trail for gospel music during the 80s. Among these were, Paradise, Paul Johnson, The Majestic Singers, Nu Colours and Lavine Hudson.

Paradise

Paradise was one of the first UK gospel groups to be signed to a record label, albeit a Christian one. Coming out of the West Indian church community, they were one of the first contemporary gospel groups in the UK. The line-up changed a number of times but mainly consisted of brothers Phil, Junior and Karlos Edwards, Bobby Clarke, Devon Burke, Victor Cross, Raymond Dennis and at different times, Doug Williams and Paul Johnson as vocalists.

Juliet Fletcher, who today heads the Gospel Music Industry Alliance, was instrumental in the early years of Paradise, first encouraging them to drop their former name, Reapers, and then signing them to her company - Oasis Management. She connected them to both Pilgrim Records and to Greenbelt, the Christian music festival. Paradise's music was groundbreaking in that it incorporated the prevailing sound of the 80s - funk music. This brought the wrath of the Black church leaders down on the group who believed they were playing 'devil's music.' They were criticised even more when they added reggae to their music.

Paradise released two albums - *Paradise* and *World's Midnight* and although neither were hugely successful, they nevertheless added to the group's growing reputation in London and on the UK Christian music scene. On the back of their growing popularity, they played a number of high-profile events including supporting Andraé Crouch at the Hammersmith Odeon, as well as appearing at Christian music festivals such as Greenbelt and at other Christian festivals in Holland and Portugal.

Paradise were real pioneers of British gospel music, and in the 80s, were one of the first British gospel groups to incorporate many of the new sounds coming out of America. They were heavily criticised for this but believed that if British gospel music were to continue, grow and develop, it should not be afraid to incorporate new sounds, styles and techniques.

Paul Johnson

Paul came from the Seventh-day Adventist Church tradition and in the late 70s and 80s was part of the early crop of gospel singers spearheading gospel music outside the Pentecostal church and into the wider community. He started singing at a young age while living in New York and came to prominence as one of the lead vocalist with Paradise. In 1987, Paul signed to CBS, recording several singles and releasing two albums, *Paul Johnson* and *Personal*. The first two singles, *When Love Comes Calling* and *Half a World Away*, was produced by Junior Giscombe, of *Mama Used to Say* fame. Paul used to be a backing vocalist for Junior, so it seemed a perfect fit.

Although neither album did well, this didn't stop Paul from carving out a successful music career for himself. He worked with several high profile artists including Bryan Ferry, Loose Ends, M People, and Incognito. He was also part of the famous 'Red Wedge Tour' headed by Billy Bragg, which in the 80s, sought to engage young people in the politics and policies of the Labour Party, with the aim of defeating the Conservatives in the General Election of 1987. Three years after the election, Paul removed himself from the music business and went into education. Today he's remembered both for his high falsetto singing and also as one of the first British gospel artists to sign to a major record label, which in the early 80s was quite an achievement.

The Majestic Singers

The Majestic Singers came out of the New Testament Church of God and, during the 70s, made a name for themselves on the gospel music circuit. Justin Lewis and Paulette Harley were the driving force behind the group which featured a young talented keyboard player - Steve Thompson. Steve later went on to work with Graham Kendrick, the hymn writer/singer of *Shine Jesus Shine* and *Servant King,* and had a great influence on his music. The Majestics also included Joel Edwards on guitar who many years later went on to head the Evangelical Alliance.

The Majestics were a group of singers, 'not a mass choir', as Paulette Harley always made clear when speaking about her 26 singers, which she and Justin Lewis hand-picked from their church organisation. In 1977 they came under the influence of Les Moir, then a recording engineer with Kingsway Music and today the A & R Executive at Integrity Music. Les recorded the group's first album, *Free at Last* with its stand-out track, *God Has Smiled on Me.* The recording helped to break the singers into the Christian music community and increased their profile both within the Black Pentecostal church community, as well as within white evangelical circles, especially with their appearances at the Greenbelt Christian Festival. The Majestics toured Europe and when American gospel artists, Jessy Dixon and Danniebelle Hall came to Britain for a concert, they were the support. They disbanded in 1984, when both Justin and Paulette left to pursue other interests.

Nu Colours

Nu Colours was Britain's premier gospel R & B group and one of its most glamorous. The group had a strong following within the Black Church Community during the 80s, especially among young people, because of the music they played and their contemporary look, which today would be considered 'cool'. The group was formed by Lawrence Johnson of London Community Gospel Choir fame and he recruited Fay Simpson, Pricilla Jones, and Lain Luther as part of the line-up. In the 1980s, the group came to the attention of Polydor Records who signed them releasing three singles, *Tears, What in the World* and *Power*. They achieved modest success with these singles, with the remixed version of *Power* being their most successful.

As well as building a reputation for themselves in the Black Church Community, in the 80s the group also built a name and a following for itself on the burgeoning UK urban music scene. Young people flocked to their concert performances as they liked the group's music and their stylish appearances. Not many people know, but they were the first gospel group to win a MOBO award and their music found support in the United States. On account of this, the group was invited to perform at the International Association of African American Music where they met Stevie Wonder and Whitney Houston. Both superstars complimented Nu Colours on their music and sound, thinking they were an American gospel group, until in Lawrence's own words, *'they heard us speak!'*

Lavine Hudson

Lavine was Britain's foremost female gospel vocalist and the resident singer on the hit television show, *People Get Ready*. She was signed to Virgin Records and for a time was touted as Britain's answer to Whitney Houston. Lavine's much anticipated album, *Intervention*, although critically acclaimed, didn't do as well as expected, despite Virgin investing heavily in it. One reason for this apparent failure was the contemporary style of the music which seemed to have alienated many people who were looking for a more traditional but modern sounding gospel album. The title track, however, did have some success in America, reaching number 19 in the R& B charts.

Virgin followed up *Intervention* with *Between Two Worlds*, again investing heavily in the album, but this time leaving the production to Rhett Lawrence, whose recording credits included James Cleveland, Andraé Crouch and The Winans, as well as top pop acts such as Mariah Carey, the Bee Gees and Barbra Streisand. Unfortunately, this didn't work either, despite Nicky Brown, Phil Collins, Phillip Bailey, and BeBe Winans adding their names and creativity to the album.

With this setback and the contraction in the music business in the early 90s, Lavine retreated to her church community in South London, where she continued with her enormous gift and talent. For many years she suffered with Lupus, which in 2017 sadly claimed her life. She will always be remembered as one of the finest female gospel vocalist, Britain has ever produced.

Gospel on Television

During the 80s television played a vital role in spreading gospel music in Britain, reflecting the growing interest in the music. The first gospel show on mainstream television was *The Rock Gospel Show* which was made by the BBC. The show was presented by Sheila Walsh - a former missionary - and by Alvin Stardust, a 1970s pop star in his own right. *The Rock Gospel Show,* was loosely based on the hugely successful *Top of the Pops* chart show, and the aim was to showcase contemporary Christian music to a mainstream audience. The problem with *The Rock Gospel Show* was that, it had more 'rock' than gospel, and was a pale imitation of *Tops of the Pops*. It was heavily criticised both within and outside of the Christian community for not being clear on what it was trying to do musically. Generally the gospel music community was disappointed with the show as it failed to capture the spirit, enthusiasm and excitement of the type of gospel music people were listening to, hearing on the radio, and seeing them on television. The show was eventually dropped.

BBC 'Songs of Praise'

BBC *Songs of Praise* is one of the longest-running programmes on British television. It has been going for over 57 years and during the 1980s, it played a vital role in bringing gospel music to a British audience. *Songs of Praise* was once a big television programme with a huge audience and would regularly pull in 7+ million viewers. It was on every Sunday evening, immediately after the early evening news and was, for many people, the nation's alternative to going to church or, as one critic put it, *'the country's religious moment.'*

On Sunday 26th February 1984, *Songs of Praise* broadcast an unusual programme from Southwark Cathedral. The programme, *A Celebration of Gospel*, was presented by Geoffrey Wheeler and produced by Christopher Mann. Along with its regular diet of hymns and interviews, *A Celebration of Gospel*, explored the background of gospel music, and featured some well-known gospel songs. The congregation was predominantly Black - which was a first for the programme - and it featured the late Sam King, who was one of the original passengers on the Empire Windrush, who arrived in Britain in 1948 but by 1984 had become Britain's first Black Mayor and the Mayor of Southwark!

A Celebration of Gospel was a big hit with the audience when it was broadcast and the programme received one of its biggest post-bags to date. It was also a watershed moment in the history of British Gospel Music, for the transmission of the programme directly led to Channel 4 commissioning TVS (Television South - formerly part of the then ITV Network), to produce a gospel music series. Andrew Barr, a former *Songs of Praise* producer, now Deputy Director of Religious Programmes at TVS, was put in charge of the series and he chose a young South African, the late Frances Tulloch, to produce the initial programmes.

People Get Ready TV Show

People Get Ready was a landmark gospel music programme and it more than any other influenced the direction and development of gospel music in Britain. As a programme, it was successful for a number of reasons. First, Andrew Barr brought several innovations to the making of the series which accounted for its success. One of these innovation was that *People Get Ready* was a partnership between TVS, the television company and the Gospel Music Community, with the production team made up of members from both.

Secondly, the series' aim was to capture the 'spirit' of a gospel church/concert event. Rather than having preconceived ideas on how to do this, Andrew relied on the advice from those of us on the production team to help him achieve this, while he and his programme-makers concentrated on the technical aspect of making each programme televisually exciting, authentic and true as possible to the music itself.

The *People Get Ready* production team consisted of Viv Broughton, Nicky Brown, Peter Toms, John Francis (presenter), Juliet Coley (presenter) and myself. As part of the production team, we had a lot of freedom to help shape the direction and content of each programme, and what we were all trying to do was to bring the excitement and experience of a gospel church service/concert, to a television audience. To do this each, programme centred on John, the singer/preacher/artist, who presented each programmes from his Hammond organ. Juliet Coley - Sister J - did the more formal television links and interviews and in the earlier programmes had her own comedy spot. Each programme included a gospel choir, a group, a soloist, short interviews and Lavine Hudson, the resident vocalist was expected to do the big show-stopping number at the end of each programme. Frances thought a lot of Lavine and was very excited when she signed to Virgin, believing that with her success, it would rub off on the series and help to make it a success.

People Get Ready used the best musicians available in the gospel community and added a top horn section to add colour, texture, and flavour. It showcased the best home-grown talent which it chose from a series of nationwide auditions which it conducted up and down the country. When I started to produce the series, we added American gospel artists to give the series an international feel. Shirley Caesar, The Williams Brothers, Tramaine Hawkins, the late Thomas Whitfield, The Oslo Gospel Choir and Larnelle Harris appeared on the show as guest artists. No amount of money was spared in making *People Get Ready* a success and TVS brought in a top Light Entertainment Director, invested heavily on the set and on both lighting, musicians and sound.

The series was a success, especially within the Black church community and today it's fondly remembered and highly spoken of. Apart from *People Get Ready*, Channel 4 also commissioned a *Gospel Christmas Special* and an original gospel oratorio, *Creation,* which was staged and filmed at the Marlowe Theatre in Canterbury.

People Get Ready was ahead of its time. If one criticism can be levied at the series which we now know in hindsight, is that we should have 'educated' the audience on the music we were presenting to win them over, as most of the music was unfamiliar to a mainstream television audience. The gospel audience knew the music, the songs and the religious content and was happy with it, but to a television audience, most of this was largely 'unknown'.

The Beginning of the End

In, the 1980s gospel music seemed to be everywhere in Britain but unfortunately like everything else, this had to come to an end. This came towards the end of the decade when economic problems appeared on the horizon, and as the economy began to contract, it led to significant changes in both society and in businesses generally. The music business was not immune to the changes in the economy with the result that the period of prosperity soon turned into a period of recession with significant falls in overall record sales. Record companies began to cut back on their spending and operations and started to lay off staff. On the Artists' side, those who were not selling 'good units' were dropped, meaning that their contracts were terminated. Unfortunately, this meant all the UK gospel artists and with this, it seemed as if the 'golden age' of gospel music had come to an end, although paradoxically the music was operating at a much higher level than before.

Gospel Music had come a long way and with this change many gospel choirs, groups and soloists were forced to disband as the work dried up and many looked for other opportunities outside of gospel music. A few did manage to find some session work but as the general work dried up, many were forced to disband and move in other directions. Many left to pursue careers, get married, start a family, while others went into the Ministry.

Not everyone, however, left gospel music altogether. Some stayed and tried to weather the storm, while others sought to reinvent themselves. Bazil Meade, for example, continued with the London Community Gospel Choir and formed a gospel music agency, extending the work of the choir to include providing music workshops, choirs for wedding, corporate events and vocal training. Noel Robinson, the main guitarist on *People Get Ready*, went solo and David Daniels, Dennis Wade, Simon Wallace and John Francis all went into the ministry, establishing successful churches and careers. I continued to pursue a television career.

PART TWO: HOW TO MAKE GOSPEL MUSIC WORK FOR YOU

(2) You Are On Your Own

The next thing to say about British gospel music is that although many artists are losing money, most are struggling with their music as well and if you're new to gospel music, you're likely to struggle too. You should take comfort however in the fact that virtually every gospel artist in Britain is more or less in the same position as you are. You may be talented, but that's not going to be enough. You may make some money, but it probably won't be as much as you think or imagine, and even if you do make any money, it's likely to be in the long term and not now. You may be 'called' to the music but you'll be frustrated and will find it difficult and hard to cope, but making gospel music can also be very rewarding. You'll also need to do everything yourself for your music and if you're not prepared to do this and not one hundred percent committed, you shouldn't bother, as this is the minimum it will take for you to get anywhere with your music.

Unlike secular artists, you won't have a record company to help you nor any record shops to sell or stock your music. There are only three radio stations that plays Christian music in the UK and only one that regularly plays Black gospel music. In all probability they're unlikely to play your CD and if you look at Christian television, the same is true for although there's more than 12 Christian channels on the Sky platform, they are all dedicated to preaching and none to gospel music.

The bottom line is that you are on your own, on your own writing the songs, sourcing the finance, sorting out the producer, and on your own doing the marketing and promotions for your music. On your own also means that you will need to acquire new skills and expertise to grow and develop your music and you will need the knowledge to do so. There's plenty of information available to help you and thankfully much of this is free, but you'll need to know where to find it, access it, and able to apply it to your music to make a success of it.

(3) Manage Your Expectations

Many gospel artists have unrealistic expectations of what their music can do and the hope they have for it is often impractical. Unfortunately, many artists who come into gospel music believe that once they've made an album or EP, all they need to do is some marketing and promotion, and with a great deal of faith, miraculously their record will sell, and they'll become successful. When this doesn't happen, and it usually doesn't, they are left feeling sad and disappointed. The problem is they have unrealistic expectations of what their music can do and really don't know what they need to do to make it successful.

Spending time and money as a new artist trying to sell your CD is likely to have only limited success. What you should do is see your CD as a marketing tool and use it as a way of building a following and an audience for your music. The more following you have, the more your followers are likely to buy from you; it's as simple as that. The only exception to this rule is if your music catches on and becomes successful - a hit. This will in itself create the demand that will enable you to sell your music. Other than that, you'll need to build a fan base for your music, for it's the supporters that you create/engage with, that will buy your CDs, which means getting fans and support for your music should be your first priority.

(4) You Will Need a Mentor and a Team Around You

One of the reasons you're likely to struggle as a new artist is because you're likely to be unknown. You may expect concert bookings and church ministries but they don't come like that.

The result of this population growth is that it has set off a chain reaction both within the Black Pentecostal church community and within gospel music itself. Today as the African population has grown, so to have their churches and African churches are now among the largest and fastest growing ones in the UK. Kingsway International Christian Centre, (KICC) is considered the single largest, while the Redeemed Christian Church of God has the most membership, estimated at around 80,000 in over 800 places throughout the country.

What this change in the Black population of Britain has shown is that almost overnight this rise in the African church population has increased the market for gospel music and now the market has a much bigger pool to draw its talent and expertise from. The market is also much more dynamic than ever before and what every gospel artist should now do is take advantage of this new development and target their music specifically to this church community for it's there they are likely to find the best support for their music.

Many gospel artists might not believe this and may seek to target their music to the general music market, or even to the White Christian market, believing this will bring them success. It's unlikely to do so for many reasons, but specifically because both markets are too broad and they lack enough buyers, who are actively seeking the music that UK artists are producing. Secondly, as most music today is niche, success is more likely to be found in these markets rather than in large mass ones. As a result of this and because of the recent demographic change, here are a few suggestions to follow if you want to succeed with your music in this market.

Treat Your Music as a Business

Although many gospel artists are happy to see their music as a ministry, few are unwilling to see it also as a business. Treating your music as a business - which you should do - will bring results but it will require a new mindset, a new approach and a new way of thinking. For some artists, seeing their music this way flies in the face of what they believe their music is for and what it represents, but if you are looking to cover your costs and make any money out of your music, you will need to bring both business and spiritual skills to it, if you are to succeed. You'll need a business plan to guide you and the business plan you choose will depend on how you see your music and the aim you have for it. With a simple business plan, what you do is set out the main areas of your music along with all its costs. At an elementary level this will tell you how much it will cost to get you going; at a more complex and professional level, your business plan will include such things as your business strategy, sales and income, balance sheet projections and cash flow analysis.

It's also likely to include systems to manage invoice payments, sales transactions, personal taxes and any financial obligations. However, whatever business plan you choose, whether it's a simple or complex one, what's important is that you have one and that it is tailored to meet the needs of your music.

Researching the Gospel Market is Essential for Success

Before starting out with your music project, it's important that you first research the type of gospel music you're going to make and the gospel market for your type of music. What does this mean? It means that by finding out as much as you can about the music you want to make and how it operates in the marketplace, you'll stand a better chance of making a success of it than if you don't. Knowledge is power and the more information you have about your music, the more you're likely to succeed with it. Research will help you make the right decision and make you less dependent on gut feelings or emotional impulses.

The more information you have about both your music and the more you know about the market for it, the more you're likely to make good decisions about your music. Information which includes the people within your market, their profile, age, level of education, occupation, the church they go to, the type of music they listen to etc., are all very useful and can help you target your music effectively. It's all about targeting your music to those who are interested in it and not about wasting your time, effort and money, trying to sell your music. It's about providing music that people want and not the music you want to give them. This is the crucial difference

Research information is always helpful, for amongst many things it will flag up opportunities when they arise and will give you an edge over your competitors. It will also help you identify the market for your music, and once you know your market, it's a matter of targeting your music there where there is a demand for it. It's not the other way around, i.e. making a record and then going out looking to see if there's a demand for it, which is what unfortunately many gospel artists tend to do. That's a 'back to front' way of doing things and is unlikely to succeed.

Word of Mouth Works - It's Essential for Success

Word of mouth is one of the most effective ways to advertise and promote your music. How often do you go to a restaurant, have a great meal and then are happy to share this information with your family and friends, who then share it with their family and friends, setting off a chain reaction? This is how word-of-mouth marketing works; one of the best and most cost-effective ways of advertising, whether it's a product, a service or gospel music. Word of mouth is handy because people trust what their family and friends say and are more likely to listen to them than any advertising. Word of mouth is such a valuable tool for it can do so much, reach so far and cost so little. It is, however, a double-edged sword, as it can equally carry good as well as bad news about your music.

Seek People of Influence to Help You With Your Music

Recommendation is another useful way of promoting your music. We rely so much today on referrals and recommendations when deciding on what to buy or who to buy from. It's because of this that websites such as Trip Advisor, Compare the Market.com and other comparison websites have become so popular. They make recommendations and referrals which we have all come to rely on. Recommendations are useful in gospel music and can be very useful to you as an artist. You should start first with your pastor who is able to bring your music to the attention of your church. Influential people and successful gospel artists can also help you, as their recommendation and endorsement is likely to carry weight. Moreover, if these influential people and artists bring your music to the attention of their supporters and followers, this can be very powerful, for it can help to get your music known and expand your own support base. Where possible, seek out DJs, TV presenters, promoters, music journalists, gospel music bloggers and people who run successful gospel music websites as these are potentially very important to your music.

Christian Radio Works

Radio promotions work, as anyone who has ever advertised knows. There are two main Christian radio stations in the UK, Premier Christian Radio and Premier Gospel. There are others including United Christian Broadcasters (UCB) and a host of internet radio stations including Cross Rhythms, Ruach Radio, UGN (Urban Gospel Network). Prayzin, Praise Radio and Revival, but the main two are Premier Radio and Premier Gospel. Both are RAJAR (Radio Joint Audience Research) registered, which means that their audiences are independently measured or audited. This means that the stations can provide specific information and profiles on who is listening to their programmes at any given time, which is very important if you are targeting your music and have limited money to spend on advertising.

Both Premier Christian Radio and Premier Gospel play gospel music, with the latter dedicated to the genre. Both offer a ready-made Christian audience of over a million listeners and both are active in London and the South East. Over 60% of the station's listeners comes from the African and Caribbean community and both probably have the best targeted audience for gospel music anywhere in the country.

The best way to get exposure on either of these stations is to buy airtime and advertise your music this way. Many gospel artists are reluctant to do this, but with the specific target that both stations offer and provide, this is a unique opportunity. Premier Gospel is geared mainly to the young, while Premier Christian Radio listeners are more of a mainstream adult Christian audience. Both stations offer a good service and if you agree to advertise with them, they are likely to throw in some add-ons and sweeteners to extend your reach. They will also offer to make your advert for you, and you should agree to this as it will make your life easy, and save you from probably falling foul of the Radio Authority's strict regulations in making religious radio advertisements if you were to make your own.

In which programmes should you advertise and how many adverts should you purchase? The 'Morning Programme', 'Drive Time' and 'Gospel Tonight' have big audiences and the amount of advertising airtime you buy will depend on who you are targeting and your budget. As an initial package to promote your music, you should look at a package that offers 30-second adverts at 4 adverts a day for 3 weeks (84), or 4 adverts a day for every other day, over a three-week period (48).

Christian Television Works Also

Contrary to popular belief, Christian television works for gospel artists promoting their music, but it only works in the strict sense in which it works on radio. For example, there are over 12 Christian Television stations on the Sky Platform and unlike Premier radio, most of them are not independently registered. BARB (Bureau of Audience Research Board) register television audiences and if a television station is not BARB registered, it's difficult to know who or how many people are watching the station's programmes. Some stations are likely to quote huge viewing figures but these are more likely to be the potential number of people in a territory available to watch a programme, rather than who is actually watching it. The station cannot know who is watching their programmes if they are not BARB registered.

This does not mean however that it's not worth advertising or promoting your music on Christian Television. On the contrary, it is, as anecdotally we know that Black Pentecostal

Christians regularly tune in to watch popular programmes that feature T.D. Jakes, Creflo Dollar, Joyce Meyer and Bishop John Francis among others. It's in these or similar programmes that you should advertise your music as they are likely to have the biggest audiences and have the type of people watching that you want to reach with your music.

Use Flyers - They Work!

One of the best things to say about flyers, especially A5 flyers, is that they work and are a great and cost-effective way for any gospel artist to promote their music. Flyers work in the Black Pentecostal Church community because people are used to them, they are affordable, and many churches and promoters use them. Flyers are an excellent way to promote your music and in the Black Pentecostal Church Community, people are likely to pick them up, read them and not throw them away. You can leave flyers almost anywhere. You can give them out at church services, at events, concerts, shopping centres, leave them in hairdressers, barber shops and cafés. They are small enough to put into a lady's handbag and small enough to fit in a man's breast-pocket. They are not cumbersome or unwieldy and are suitable for door-to-door drops. They can even be inserted in periodicals and magazines. To make your flyer effective, you should ensure that it is well designed, well printed, and that it has a clear message to tell. If you want it to have an impact and stand out from among the plethora of other flyers, make sure that yours is attractive and engaging, as there is no end to where your flyer can go to carry the message about your music.

Christian Publications Work Too

Historically, *The Voice* newspaper and its *'Soul Stirring'* page edited by Marcia Dixon, was once the leading and influential publication for gospel music in the UK. Other publications like *Cross Rhythms* have been profiling gospel artists and their music for years as have other publications like *Nu Nation, Pride Magazine, The Gleaner, Spread the Word,* (now online) and some other lesser-known publications. Today, there are only two publications that regularly feature gospel music; *Soul Stirring* and *Keep the Faith,* with the latter now the dominant publication in the market place. There are other publications within the broader Christian community such as *The Church Times, Christians Today, War Cry* (The Salvation Army), *The Methodist Recorder* and *Christianity*, which will publish the odd story on UK Gospel music but you'll need to approach them with a good story to stand any chance of getting anything published. A conversion story may all be well and good, but these publications are likely to want something more journalistic, so have your story ready before you approach them to write anything about your music.

them on an album and with plenty of prayers and fasting and a bit of promotion, their album will sell and it will do well. It won't, for you'll need to know how gospel music sells in the UK, who are the buyers and where they are located. If you're going to succeed with your music, you're going to need the knowledge to match your spirituality plus the practical demands of knowing how to make your music work for you.

It's not just about making music, if it ever was, nor is it about putting the music out in the market place and hope that people will hear it, like it and want to buy it. It doesn't work that way. It's about knowing the music people are looking for and providing them with this, rather than offering them the music you want to give them, however good you think your music may be. This is the vital difference! Using social media can help you but you will need to know how social media works in relation to music to get the best out it and not simply how it works on a personal level.

(5) Grow Your Fan Base to Grow Your Music

Today gospel artists have many opportunities to get their music known but rather than do this they spend their time trying to sell their CDs, hoping understandably, to see a return on their investment. What they don't realise is that they are going about this the wrong way. As a gospel artist, especially a new one, initially you should not spend your time trying to sell your CD, but spend it building and growing a following and a fan base for your music.

For example when starting out, it's unlikely that you'll be known or will have the support you'll need to get your music off the ground. What you should do is start to build a following for your music. Social media is a good place to start, as is using a mailing list, starting a blog, sending out newsletters and using a host of other fan base building initiatives.

Growing a fan base or an audience for your music will call for a new mindset and a new way of thinking. Merely making an album/EP and placing some information about it online is not enough. Millions of albums/EPs are uploaded every minute on line and what will make yours stand out and get noticed? Today the received wisdom is that if you're a new independent artist and want to succeed with your music, start to build a fan base. You can begin with your family and friends, and extend this to include members of your church, people in your college, university, etc. From there you can spread your net out to include other supporters of your music, people in the same line of music as you are and those who have an influence in your market-place. Growing a fan base should be your priority and it should feature prominently in your business plan.

(6) You'll Find the Best Support for Your Music in Black Pentecostal Churches

Like its American counterpart, UK Gospel music is deeply rooted in a Black Pentecostal church tradition and it's from there that it draws its inspiration and strength. Not too long ago in Britain this church community was mainly Caribbean, but since the turn of the century, it's predominantly African. What this change has done is to inject 'new blood' into the music, increased the market for it and has widened the pool from where it draws its talent and support. Black Pentecostal churches are the natural home for gospel music and the place where you as a gospel artist should target your music if you want to see it grow and develop. More gospel music than ever is being produced in Britain today and the market is lively and buoyant. African artists now represent the most significant area of growth in the music and African churches are now the dominant force. African churches have the largest congregations and offer the main audience for the music. While you may think that you should target other denominations with your music, it's in the Black Pentecostal Churches that you'll find the best support for your music and the place where you're likely to get the best results. How to get your music into these churches is the challenge you'll face.

Before you start, you'll need to do some research and decide on a plan. You'll need to know how these churches work, understand their psychology, know what music works in these churches and, importantly, who the 'main players' are. In most cases this is the pastor and people on the leadership team of the church, including the music director if the church has one. You'll need to build relationships with the pastors and music ministers and develop a strategy if you're to stand a chance of getting your music into any of these churches.

It's not also about sending your music to them either, for that doesn't work. It's about seeking to give these churches the music that they want and not what you want them to hear. This is the crucial difference. If you do this, your music is likely to be welcomed in African churches.

(7) Pastors Hold the Key to Your Success

One of the most significant changes that have taken place in British gospel music in recent years is the role that pastors now play in the music. In the absence of a credible gospel infrastructure, pastors, many with large congregations, have now become both A&R *(artist and recording)* managers and de facto gospel promoters. They are now the new gatekeepers of the music as it is they who decide on who performs in their churches and to their congregations. Pastors now occupy this default position, and because they have the numbers, the finance, and the venues, they've become very powerful, not only in their own right but increasingly over the music itself. This is the new reality and every gospel artist who want to succeed with their music and make it work for them, will need to know this and ultimately seek to convince pastors to let them into their churches with their music. Failure to do so is likely to severely restrict an artist growth of their music.

One of the things you will need to do as an artist to get your music into African churches, is to get African pastors to know about you and your music. To do this, you'll need to raise your profile within gospel music and within African Churches. Social media can help you, as most African pastors are social media savvy and often look to this medium to help them decide who to have in their churches to minister and perform. Building a relationship with a pastor's wife, the music minister or any member of the church leadership team is a way that can also help you to get to the pastor who usually makes the final decision.

Until recently, African pastors were content to invite American gospel artists into their churches to minister and perform and although many still do, they are increasingly turning to their own artists as some of them have become popular and their congregations are singing these artists songs. Both Muyiwa/ Riversongz, Sinach, Lara George, and Nathaniel Bassey are good examples of African artists whose songs are popular in African churches and as a consequence, they are frequently invited to minister and perform in African churches.

(8) Pastors Are Your Best Friend

If you are a new gospel artist, you should know that your album promotion and its potential success probably lies with pastors and that they are likely to be your best friend if you're able to build a relationship with them. This means that before you even start your album/EP project, you should first reach out to your pastor to get him/her on board. There are some simple things that you can do to help you get your pastor marketing and promotional materials that you use. How active your brand is will depend on how well you promote your music as this can make all the difference between being known or remaining anonymous.

There may be some parts of your brand that are more significant than others, but you should aim to make your brand holistic, able to attract people and make your music consistently recognisable. Always seek to promote your brand and get it known. Merely having a good album or an excellent EP, is not enough as you'll need the right image, a particular style and a consistent identity that will stand out and get you noticed in what is often a very crowded gospel music marketplace. Your brand should say everything about you and your music and should be the experience people have when they come into contact with you. Your brand is all-encompassing, it's you, your music and everything in between.

(14) Your Website is the Shop Window to Your Music

As an artist, your website is the shop window to your music and the visual representation of your ministry and brand. You should make sure that your site is the best that it can be, that it is regularly updated, has useful and relevant content, along with good quality photos. When someone visits your website, it should be clear who you are, what your music is about and it should say, look and feel the music that you are portraying. You should make sure that your site is professional, accessible and easy to read. The more professional it is, the better the impression it will give. It should also look like a music website and not some corporate blue chip one, excellent though this may be, for that's not the point. You are about music and your site should reflect this, making visitors feel comfortable and at ease when they visit your site, knowing that they are where they expect to be and not somewhere else.

Think carefully also about the colours you use, for this is very important. Colours have emotional meaning, association and appeal, and it's essential that your site and the colours of your social media pages reflect your music and the meaning you're trying to convey. Think how major brand use colours. Can you imagine a yellow tin of Coke or Facebook coloured purple? We associate Coke with red and Facebook with blue and white. Why these colours? The same is also true if you are targeting young people where colours are very important and can make all the difference. Look at any website that appeals to young people, and what do you see but bright youthful colours - why is this?

(15) Record Traditional Songs, for they Work

Traditional songs are songs and tunes which are known and performed by a community over many years, sometimes over many generations. They are often songs which represent the history and culture of a people and in many cases, many of the writers are unknown, which mean that the songs are likely to be in the public domain, out of copyright and usually free to record. Where these songs are useful to gospel artists, is when they are given a new treatment and brought back to life as a new song. This is what Donnie McClurkin did with his *Live in London* CD and his Caribbean medley.

The medley on the album are traditional choruses which Caribbean churches have been singing for years. What Donnie did was to record a few of these and by giving them a new treatment and sound, brought them to life on the album, and it is this which many people believe gives the album its distinctive appeal and accounts for its enormous success. Edwin Hawkins did the same thing in 1968 with *Oh Happy Day*, and nearer our time, this is what Nathaniel Bassey has done with *Imela*, taking a traditional African gospel song,

Arranging your songs beforehand will make it easier for producers to do what you are paying them to do, which means bringing all their creative and production skills to bear on your songs to make them the best they can be. The more time a producer has to do this, the better the chances of getting a good result. Your producer's time should be spent producing your songs and not spending your studio time in arranging them. My suggestion is that unless a producer offers to arrange your songs, you should get them arranged first before taking them to be recorded, for it will save you time and money.

Choose the Right Producer

The producer is the person who is responsible for the technical and creative side of any recording, including the mixing and mastering. They are ultimately responsible for how your music sounds, and it's therefore important that you choose the right person to produce your music and songs. There's no right or wrong way to do this, but a producer who has a good record of successfully producing the type of music that you are looking for, makes sense. To do a good job requires a great deal of skill and experience and it's the combination of this, a balance between the songs that you bring, the budget that you have and the skills that a producer brings to your project, that will account for its success.

Once you've decided on a producer, you should arrange a meeting to discuss your songs and to talk about the recording. If the producer make some suggestions and you are happy with them, you should take them on board. If not, you should say what you think and say what you'd like and what you are looking for. Be sensible though and don't try to fit a square peg into a round hole for you'll regret it. Don't forget also that it is you who is paying for the recording, and what you are doing is hiring the skills of a producer to deliver a good outcome for you. This means that you should be clear on what you want and that you are happy with your producer and that both of you are agreed on the outcome you are looking for.

This may seem an obvious point, but it's worth checking that the producer has the necessary skills, experience, and creative ability to interpret your music the way you hear it and is able to deliver a good outcome for you. Be careful as there's plenty of hype and many producers have inflated egos and are not as experienced as they make out, nor do they have the track record to show for it. If you are not sure or feel uncomfortable or you don't think the producer is capable, or the producer is charging too much, you should find another one even if the one you've chosen is well-known. If you are in two minds and don't know what to do, you can always suggest doing a single track to see how you both get on, and if you're happy with the result, this may encourage you to proceed. What you should never do is to overstretch yourself financially and always keep in mind that your recording is merely one of a series you intend to make. Remember, Rome wasn't built in a day and an oak tree was once an acorn; you have time to grow and develop, so take your time and don't be in a hurry.

Draw Up a Simple Recording Agreement

Once you have agreed on a producer, and the producer is in place, the next step is to write up a simple 'Letter of Agreement'. This is not as difficult as it may sound and there are plenty examples online to help you. You don't need a complicated agreement or contract either but a simple letter that sets out what you and the producer have agreed to do. You - to pay for the recording - and the producer - to 'record', 'mix' and 'master' your songs and deliver the 'mixed master recording' to you at an agreed date. Make sure you include in the agreement that you want to 'agree on each track before it is committed to the mix', so that you have a say on the final outcome of each track. Try as much as possible however, to build a good relationship with your producer, for this will benefit your music. The reverse unfortunately, is equally true.

Payment Schedule

Once you have set out the general terms of your recording in the agreement, include a 'payment schedule' section. In this section you should show the total amount of money you've agreed to pay the producer, including all ancillary costs, You should also state how you intend to pay for the recording. While many gospel producers are happy with 50% of the costs payable in advance and the balance payable on completion, like anything, this is negotiable and is a matter of what you and the producer agrees.

A much better arrangement is 30% of the cost payable at the start of the recording, 30% at a set date in the middle, and the balance on delivery. This type of arrangement has the advantage of allowing you to spread your payments and perhaps more importantly, it gives you some control over your money in the event of anything going wrong.

Whatever you do, do not pay all the money upfront or in advance.

Once you've agreed the terms of the Recording Agreement, you and the producer should both sign and date it, with each keeping the other's signed copy for safekeeping. Naturally, like anything else, for you to have a good recording experience, it will depend on the relationship you have with your producer. Try to build a good relationship, for this will help to ensure a good outcome for your recording.

THE RECORDING
Album or an EP (extended play)?

One of the first things you will need to decide as a gospel artist is whether to record an album or an EP. At its most basic, an album is a collection of songs that is put together by a number of processes in a recording studio. The songs can either be recorded live with instruments, or made with computer-generated sounds, or a mixture of both. Most gospel artist music in Britain is computer generated music, record in home studios with the vocals recorded live. With computer-generated music, there's no need for live instruments as this only adds to the cost. However, if you want to make a genuinely authentic sounding gospel album/EP, you should record it in a professional studio and use live instruments, but it's a matter of choice and a person's ability to pay. Music professionally recorded in a studio with live instruments will always sound better than music which is computer generated but this is expensive, and not everyone can afford it. Computer-generated music with live vocals is what most new gospel artists use as their first recording and it is an excellent and well-acknowledged way to begin a music career.

How Much Should I Pay for my Recording?

In the UK, a gospel album generally consists of between 10 and 12 tracks (songs) and a 'good' producer charges, on average, anywhere between £500 and £750+ per track, although they can and do charge more. This means a 12-track album at £500 per track will cost £6,000, and one at £750 per track will cost £9,000.

In the UK, gospel albums sell at around £10.00 each which mean that for an artist to break even on a 12 track album costing £6,000 to record, they will need to sell 600 CDs to recoup on the recording cost alone. On a recording that costs £9,000, they will need to sell 900 CDs. Trying to sell these numbers in the UK as a new artist is hard and if graphic design, pressing, marketing and promotion costs are added, the overall cost increase substantially, making it perhaps prohibitive to make. You may be surprised to know that even established gospel artists in the UK struggle to make anything like these numbers!

Recording an EP is a much better option and a good starting point for any new gospel artist. At its most basic, a gospel EP (extended play) is generally, although not exclusively, music that is computer-generated with the vocals recorded live. On average in the UK, an EP consists of three or four songs and although EPs can have live instruments, it is unusual. The cost of recording an EP can vary widely, anywhere between £300 and £500 per track. This means that a three track EP at £300 per track will cost £900 and one at £500 per track will cost £1,500.

In the UK, gospel EPs sells at around £6 so it will take 150 CDs and 250 CDs to break-even on the recording cost of £900 and £1,500 respectively. Even at this level, when design, pressing, marketing and promotion costs are added, making an EP is still not cheap, but it's far more cost effective than recording an album. Recording an EP also has the advantage of allowing an artist to grow their music incrementally rather than risking all their money in one go and perhaps invariably failing.

Gospel albums sell better in the UK than EPs, but the cost of recording an album, getting it pressed, plus the marketing and promotions are all very costly, so recording an EP is still a much better option and by far a more cost-effective alternative. Some gospel artists who are established and have a strong following might find making an album more appropriate to their needs and if this is the case, they should follow what's best for them and do what will bring them a return on their investment.

The Mix

Mixing is the process in a recording cycle in which the producer and engineer put all the different recorded tracks together and musically blend them into one complete musical whole, creating the best possible sound in the process. Mixing is a skilful art and although all the recording processes are important, how a track is 'mixed' can make or break a track. For example, a track that is well recorded and poorly mixed is likely to fail, while a track that is mixed well, can turn out to be a great track. Mixing is critical to any recording and in some cases, especially in the secular world, once a track or an album is recorded, another producer or an experienced mixer who has a speciality in this area is brought in to do the mix. The new person is likely to bring their own creativity, and a fresh ear to the mix and may be able to add something 'special' to make the recording great. Most gospel artists are content to leave the mixing to their producer, and while this is fine, make sure that you have a chance to hear each track - as per your agreement - before they are mixed and mastered to avoid any disappointment.

Mastering

This is the last stage in the recording process and at its most straightforward it involves editing the recorded tracks, making sure that all the sounds and levels are correct and in their right places. It also involves removing all extraneous noises in the recording and making any minor adjustments.

Metadata

One of the most critical pieces of information that every gospel artist should now insist on and make sure that it is included in their recording agreement, is the inclusion of the 'metadata' of each song. Metadata is the identifying information that you should make sure is embedded in the computer files of all your recorded tracks. The metadata provides the information that identifies both your album or EP, and each of the songs. It also includes a range of other useful information such as the title of the song, the composer, all the performers on the track, the year the song was released, the track number if it's an album or EP, the genre of the song/EP, the producer and the lyrics. It can even contain the artwork of the album/EP.

Once the metadata is embedded in your recording, it will show up on the music business central databases such as Rovi, All Music and Gracenote, which are the websites music professionals use to check the status of recordings or to find information on any song that's recorded. These sites are also the place where radio stations, collection agencies, performing rights organisations and licensing authorities go to find information on music they are looking for. Increasingly it's also the way social media now rank pages on their sites, and the way the world is moving as more and more devices use smart technology.

The Stems

This is a crucial stage in the recording process and a point that has caused and continues to cause many problems for UK gospel artists. Generally, gospel artists tend to find it difficult to get their 'Stems' after their recording. 'Stems' are all the materials associated with a recording ie the multi-channel audio files, and sub-mixes. **These Belong to You the Artist**

and Not the Producer, and by right they should be returned to you after the recording. To make sure that this happens, include this in your recording 'letter of agreement'. Here is an example of what you could include about the return of your stems.

"I (name of artist) request it to be known that the producer (name) has no right whatsoever to any of the songs in this recording. Furthermore, all the recording files and audio stems as this is known and understood in the music business and elsewhere and used in the recording is the property of the artist (your name) and that the producer (name) agrees to return these to (artist name) within five days of the recording."

10

Now You've Made Your Album/EP, What Next?

Listing Songs/Track Order

Now that you've made a gospel album/EP, embedded the metadata, and you have your stems returned, the next step is to get your CDs pressed, but before doing that, you'll need to decide on the order of your songs and how your CD is going to look. Listing songs for an album and the order in which you list them will depend on what you think will make the album work, what you like, or even what takes your fancy. Record companies are quite good at listing songs for an album because they've doing it for years and likely to know the order of songs that will make an album work. It's unlikely that you as a gospel artist will have this kind of experience, so here are a few tips to help you.

The first thing you should do when listing songs for your album/EP, is to ask yourself the question, who am I listing the album/EP for. You are not listing for yourself or listing what takes your fancy, but listing for your audience. Your audience mean the people who will listen to your CD and ultimately will want to buy it. You should have them uppermost in your mind when putting the order of your songs together.

Try to work out different permutations and make each one flow smoothly without jarring. Think how your buyers and customers will hear the songs and try to make them 'flow' as an overall, unified listening experience.

Think about the mood and feel you want to create. If you want to create a happy/lively, jolly feeling, you should put your up-tempo songs at the top of the list, adding the slow ones for pace and balance. If it's a slow, moody, worshipful introspective feel you are trying to create, the order you list your songs should reflect this, with the up-tempo numbers added for balance, contrast and variety. Remember also that people's attention span is very short, and so try to engage your listeners as quickly as possible and keep them interested as long as you can, otherwise they're likely to become uninterested. It's better in this sense to put your 'best songs' at the top of your album/EP rather than towards the end. If the tracks are good, they are likely to get people's attention straight away rather than turning them away, knowing the best songs are at the end.

The same is equally true if your CD has three or 12 songs. On a three-track EP if the feeling you want to create is an up-tempo one, then you should list your up-tempo songs as your first songs with a slow song in the middle to give it balance and perhaps end with another up-tempo number. The opposite will also work for a 'worshipful', reflective EP of three songs, with the slow songs as the first and second track, with a moderately up-tempo number at the end for balance. Three slow songs can also work, but it's mostly a matter of experience and a general feel for the audience. What's important however is to have 'great songs', for with 'great songs' they tend to list themselves.

CD Design

Once your songs are recorded, mixed, mastered and listed, the next step is to think about the design of your CD. This is the graphic design stage of your project and one which is very important. You should think carefully about this stage and take it seriously if you want people to engage with you and buy your music. Your CD is likely to be the first thing that anyone will see when they come into contact with your music, and the first thing they are likely to judge you by. This means that your CD design should make a good impression, for it's likely to be a lasting one. This is particularly true in the Black Pentecostal church community where people like the physical copy of a CD, and though CDs sales are falling elsewhere, in this community, CDs still sell. You should also make sure that your CD is well designed and hire a professional graphic designer to help with your design rather than you and your friends try to do this yourself. Finding a professional graphic designer shouldn't be difficult as there are plenty on the internet offering their services. If however you're in doubt, you can always ask your fellow gospel artists to recommend one to you.

When hiring a graphic designer, you will need to put a 'brief' together. This is a written explanation/instruction on the ideas you have in mind for your CD design. To do this properly, you should do some research beforehand on CD covers and it's worth going to record stores to look at CDs on display, looking in your own CD collection, researching the internet and also looking in art and photographic galleries for inspiration. Research also the font you want to use as this can make all the difference to your design and choose one that is current and not out of date, unless stylistically it's part of the design that you want to achieve. Always use good quality photographs and ask your graphic designer to let you know what resolution they need to be.

Once you've decided on the ideas for your design, write this up as a 'brief' and give as much information as possible. Once you've done this, send it to your graphic designer but remember that what you write is merely a guide, so be sensible and do not write reams and reams of useless information.

In the UK, gospel CD designs are not always that inspiring although there are exceptions and many are getting better. The problem is that many CD designs are bereft of any real artistic merit and too many are littered with clichéd images that dominates their designs. These include the usual ascending and descending white angels, rolling clouds, doves, the obligatory eagle, and that all-embracing lion. I know what Pentecostal graphic artists are trying to say with these images, but they are overused, passé, with not enough thought given to how these images can be used creatively, to produce good designs.

UK gospel graphic artists need to up their game in this area as their designs are competing for the attention of buyers who are themselves continually being bombarded with great images and designs, all vying for their attention. What gospel graphic designers should do is to make sure that their illustrations and designs are modern, relevant, contemporary and spiritually uplifting. They should always have in their mind that their role is to visually convey with their design, the thinking and meaning behind an artist's music, and that it should sit comfortably alongside the best designs that are in the marketplace.

Above all, seek to build a relationship with your graphic designer for this will help you get the best result for your CD. Remember that you get the designer you choose, and that you're likely to get what you pay for.

How Many CDs to Press

Anecdotally, UK gospel artists tend to press far too many CDs which they are unable to sell. How many CDs you should press is a debatable point and will depend on how many copies you believe you can sell or how many you need to sell to break-even and cover your costs. If you are coming into the market for the first time, or if you want to test your music's appeal, you should consider a short run of between 100 and 200 CDs. What's good about a short run is that it's manageable and gives you control and you can always top up your stock as the demand for your music increases. With large runs, you run the risk of losing your of money because you are unable to sell the number of CDs you've pressed - so be careful.

Short runs may not be good for every gospel artist and it's true that some artists who have a large support base may want to press more than 200 CDs. That's fine and every gospel artist should do what works for them. On the whole though, short runs make sense and as gospel CDs have a long shelf life, you can always continue to sell them long after their release date, giving you the chance to recoup on your investment.

CD Duplication vs Replication

When getting your CD pressed, you should get them 'duplicated' rather than 'replicated'. CD 'duplication' works on the same principle as a person burning information or data onto a blank CD, while 'replication' is where the information or data is added to a 'Master CD' during the manufacturing process, and it's from this 'Master,' that copies are 'replicated' - made. Most gospel artists in the UK have their CDs duplicated because with this process they can order small quantities, whereas, with replication, the minimum order is likely to be anywhere between 1,000 and 2,500 CDs.

Barcode

If you want to have your CDs available in shops, retail outlets, digital music platforms, or even possibly enter the gospel music charts, you will need to make sure that they have a bar code to help you track their sales. Getting a bar code is a simple process, and most good graphic artists offer this as part of their service. Ask yours about this.

Register Your Songs

Once you have recorded and pressed your CDs, the next step is to register your songs. Technically, you should have done this before you recorded them and both PRS (Publishing Rights Society) and the MCPS (Mechanical Copyright Protection Society) websites offer and provide ways for you to do this. Join them and as a member, you'll also be able to collect any royalties that may be due to you when your EP/Album is released.

COLLECTING ROYALTIES

PRS –Publishing Rights Society

PRS collects royalties on behalf of songwriters, composers and artists signed to publishers. It also collects royalties on behalf of its members whenever their songs are played or performed in public. Copyright is the exclusive right provided to the owner of an original creative work. This means that if you have written an original song, and it is played on Christian radio or on any radio station for that matter, or it is aired on Christian television or any television station, then you should be entitled to royalties providing that you have registered the song. The same is also true if your song is performed or played in public, whether it's in a venue, concert hall, shop, or is played as a digital download or as streamed music. There are a few exceptions; for example, if your song is played in a hospital, in an old people's home or in a church service, (not a concert), but on the whole, if your song is played on the air and performed in a public place, you're likely to be entitled to royalties.

Only artists who write their songs or have written them jointly need to register with PRS. If you have written a song together with another person, each of you should join PRS separately as writers, if you want to be able to collect the royalty that is due to you. To register as a member, go to www.prs.com/royalties, and register. You'll be able to manage your account online, check royalty payments, amend works, claim unpaid royalties and report live performances.

MCPS – Mechanical Copyright Protection Society

This organisation represents songwriters, composers and music publishers. MCPS collects and distributes royalties on music whenever it is reproduced as a physical product whether it's a CD, digital download, DVD or whether it is broadcast online, on TV, the radio, websites or in feature films. MCPS collects royalties by issuing licences to music users regarding the mechanical copyright in musical works. It is known as a collecting society because its primary role is to collect money from people or organisations that use its members' music.

PPL – Phonographic Performance Limited (ppluk.com)

PPL is a royalty collection organisation useful to anyone who has performed on recorded music. PPL pays the performer on songs as if they are a record company that owns the recordings. To become a member of PPL is free and any gospel artist releasing an album/EP should register as both a 'Performer' and as a 'Rights Holder', as PPL is able to collect royalties for both roles.

CCLI - Christian Copyright Licensing International

CCLI is a Christian songwriters' organisation that looks after Christian songwriters and work to make sure that Christian music both nationally and internationally is used legally and that its members are paid fairly for their work. CCLI partners with labels, publishers, churches and Christian organisations to ensure that Christian artists' songs are adequately protected by the law. CCLI also make the work of Christian artists accessible and attainable to audiences throughout the world.

Gospel Music Video

Now that you have recorded your songs, designed and pressed your CD and made sure that your songs are registered, the next stage is to shoot your music video. A music video is a visual representation of the song you want to promote from your album or EP. In the music business, this is usually the 'single' which a record company generally uses to get an artist known.

How a music video is made is through a combination of camera shots, angles, locations, performances and a range of visual know-how. The aim is that once an audience sees your video, they'll remember the song and remember you. How well a music video is made will depend on the creative and artistic skills of the Video Director. A good music video can make a good song a hit while a lousy video can destroy a song. The lesson here is choose your video director with care, similarly as you would with a record producer.

On the whole, gospel videos in the UK have significantly improved over the years and they are continuing to do so. There are some excellent gospel music videos, but there's always room for improvement. One concern is that video directors are still not paying enough attention to syncing the pictures to the music. There's too much 'goldfishing' as it's known in the business. This is where a person singing is not entirely in sync with the music, leading to the singer acting like a goldfish - continually opening and closing their mouth, with nothing coming out!

Another area of concern is the high cost of making gospel videos. Making a gospel video in the UK is very expensive, anecdotally anything between £3,000 and £5,000 on average. Given the low return on CD sales, this investment is disproportionally high and although it's understandable why video directors feel they need to charge this amount, it's difficult to see how artists can recoup on the cost on their music videos from CD sales alone. A lyric video is a much cheaper alternative which you should consider.

Another approach you can make when deciding on a video director, given how expensive they are, is to look for one straight out of media college and who is looking for opportunities to display their directorial skills. It's likely that these video directors are young and bursting with exciting ideas and are looking for opportunities. Seek them out, for this is likely to save you money and this might be just what you need to make your video stand out.

The Video Agreement

If you decide to use a Video Director, whether established or out of college, you should make sure that you have a written agreement with them. At a simple level, you can base this on your recording agreement but remember to add that the director, (name) 'has no legal right to your video and that all, 'out-takes' and 'rushes' should be returned to you after the video has been edited'. This is to make sure that you keep all the footage as this rightly belongs to you as you've paid for it! It doesn't belong to the video director unless you have specifically agreed to this. You should also make sure that every person who appears in your video signs a 'release form' or letter stating that they also have no legal right or claim to your video.

The same is also true where you shoot your video. If, for example, you shoot a scene outside a person's business and you have not cleared this with the owner; if the business is visible in your video and is seen as a part of it, the owner can legally object to your video being shown and/or insist that you remove the scene with his/her building, or you pay for the privilege of keeping it in the video. You have been warned!

What Makes a Good Gospel Music Video

What makes a good video is the same as asking what makes a good song. There's no definite answer, and any attempt is purely subjective. There are, however, a few tips which you might find useful when making your music video. To start with, your music video is the visual representation of your music, song and brand, and an indication of how you want to be seen and how you want people to view you and your music. You should make sure your video is well shot, imaginative, innovative, has an excellent storyboard, and is well-edited, leaving the viewer with an enjoyable and memorable feeling and experience.

Approach your music video in much the same way as you approach the design of your CD, researching the idea you have for it. Don't forget there are hundreds, even thousands, of music videos inside and outside of gospel music to help you and act as inspiration. Choose the video director carefully as there's no substitute for a good director. A good director can make all the difference to your video, bringing skill, experience and expertise to what you are doing and in the process make your music visually appealing.

There are some other simple tips to bear in mind. If, for example, your song is a happy, joyous and an uplifting number, then it's perhaps best to shoot your video outside on location to make use of natural light. You should ask for it to be edited with 'fast cuts' and 'dissolves' to give it tempo and pace.

It's important that your video reflects the message and mood of your song. If for example your song is a worship number, then the video should reflect the mood/feel and emotions that the song portrays. Slow, tracking shots accompanied by big close-ups along with good quality camera work and sensitive lightening tend to work best and here it's perhaps best to avoid daylight locations.

Where possible, tell your video director to avoid stereotypical gospel and religious shots, which means staying clear of pastoral scenes, fields with flower beds, waterfalls, doves and an over-reliance on clouds whether rolling or static as they have all been overdone. Humour is always good in any video, so keep things light and don't try to 'over sing' which so many gospel artists tend to do, spoiling their videos. Sing naturally and let the director and the camera do the work and always remember, that less is more, and that which is unusual, engaging, off the wall, out of the box, or even shocking, can attract attention, so make your video memorable, allowing it to stand out and leave a lasting impression.

Your Music Video and YouTube

Once you've shot your video, like most people, you're likely to head straight to YouTube to upload it. Merely uploading and leaving it there with no marketing and promotions behind it, is like getting into a car with no petrol and expecting it to move. There are thousands, even hundreds of thousands, of music videos uploaded every minute on YouTube, so how will yours stand out and get noticed? Here, 'get noticed' means, to stand out and get noticed in the marketplace for your music - your target audience - and not among the millions of people watching YouTube. One way to do this is to have a great video of a great gospel song that it is well produced, well shot and is visually pleasing enough to attract attention. Another way is to target your video directly to where people are looking for the type of song that you have made, and if your song is a 'cover,' viewers are more likely to respond to a song that they know than one they don't know. This is why recording a 'cover' makes sense but you will need to follow up your music video with a robust marketing and promotional campaign. Above all, remember that YouTube is not a retail outlet but a social media platform and it is an excellent tool to market and promote your music, so use your music video to engage with people online, rather than trying to use it to sell your CD, as this rarely works.

11

Your Music and Social Media - 1

Social media has changed all our lives, and for many people, it's now all the rage. Social media has opened the world in a way no one could ever have imagined or foreseen. Anyone today with an internet connection can join with people all over the world and share their stories, photos, and messages, and can do this all with a few clicks of a mouse. Social media has also changed the way we engage with each other, changed the way businesses engage with their customers and the way governments communicate with voters. It's truly a revolutionary way of communicating and has given a new meaning to the term 'to engage'.

Today there are many social media sites with millions of people engaging with them every day. Few people are unaffected by this and millions cannot imagine a life without social media. Even in the entertainment world, social media has changed the way record companies now operate. Who would have thought a few years ago before digital technology, the internet, Pro Tools and social media, that anyone who wanted to make a record could do so? Only record companies were able to do this as they had the know-how, resources and distribution network. Now today anyone with relatively little money can make a record and with social media, have it in front of a global audience in a matter of seconds. Fans too who were once distant from their artists, and would only see them in concerts, on the television and hear them on the radio, can now engage with them regularly online in a new symbiotic relationship, with social media both the creator and catalyst of this engagement.

At its core, social media is a place where interaction takes place and a place where you as an artist can engage with followers and fans to develop and grow your music. With social media you should aim to build a following and a support base for your music. To do this, you will first need to identify the people who are interested in your music and know where to find them. Once you have this information, you can begin to target your music directly to this group - your target audience - as this is where you're likely to find the best support for your music. It's not about promoting your music everywhere, whether on or off-line, but targeting it specifically to people who are interested in your music, as these are your potential 'followers,' 'supporters' and fans.

Social media is a tool which you should use to promote your music but to do this effectively it's important to know the basic elements of how social media works as regards music promotions to get the benefit from it. 'Engagement' is everything on social media and it's a recurring theme, but to engage effectively with your target audience, you'll need to be clear as an artist on the identity of your music and make it easy to be recognised. Demographic information can help you get to know your target audience and thankfully most social media sites have this information. For example, if you're on Facebook and Instagram, both sites can tell you who is interested in your music, who are your potential followers, who's following you, where they are located, their age, sex, gender and a host of other useful information. With this information you're in a much better position to know who to pitch your music to and where to seek out 'friends' and engage with followers. Notice that this has nothing to do with trying to sell your music, as this will come later. At this stage it's all about seeking friends online and engaging with them.

One of the simplest ways to start to build support for your music is to start with people you know, people who are interested in you and your music and those in the same line of music as you are. In the first instance, these are likely to be your family, your friends, people in your church and other artists in your field. This doesn't mean targeting everyone in gospel music, as this is too broad a reach. You'll need to be more specific, even forensic and target people who are interested in the music that you make - your specific genre of gospel music. Facebook is a great place to start as it is the dominant player in the marketplace with over 2 billion users and over 40 million active users in the UK.

Facebook

Today Facebook is where most social interaction takes place online and where the highest number of people go to meet, make friends, share messages, information, photos and videos. It's an essential platform for any gospel artist wishing to grow their music but it doesn't mean that because Facebook has a vast audience all you have to do as an artist is post information about your music on the site, or upload your music video and people will come rushing to engage with you and buy your CD. They won't, the site doesn't work like that and if you think it does, you're going to be disappointed. Facebook is a social media platform and you should always see it and use it that way. Your aim on Facebook should be to build a following bringing people into your 'friendship loop'. By engaging with them, they'll become your fans, support your music, eventually buy from you and champion you and your music to their friends and followers, and eventually the world!

(i) Make your Artist Facebook Page attractive

One of the first things you should do on Facebook is to make your Profile page the best that it can be. Your Profile page is the place where you should provide precise information about you and your music. It is the place where anyone visiting your page, will get a chance to know who you are and be able to read all about you and your music. It's a mirror to your music and therefore you should make sure that it looks good, has good quality photos, is interesting, meaningful, easy on the eye, and it leaves a lasting impression. It's not a page for your personal activities unless it relates to your music and as such you should avoid posting pictures of dinners with your friends, nights out with the girls, taking the dog for a walk or any such similar activities. Steer clear also of posting images, photos and videos of your family, friends, pets etc, in fact anything that's not connected to your music should not be posted, for this is likely to give the impression that you are not a serious artist.

(ii) Facebook is about attracting 'followers'

One way to attract 'followers' to your Facebook page is to start a conversation on the site or join an existing one. Posting regular and consistent information, comments, pictures, photos and videos will help you do this, as these provides opportunities for people to respond to your posts and this will enable you to start a conversation with them. Where the discussion will lead will depend on the regularity and consistency of your engagement and the depth of the relationship that you are able to build with those who engage with you.

(iii) It's also about building a following

Facebook is about engagement. Engagement in this sense is an interaction; a two-way conversation flow between you as an artist and the 'followers' you attract who are interested in you and your music. You should aim to get people to 'like' and 'share' what you post. Initially, you may have to offer some incentives and inducements which could mean your CD, signed photographs, free concert tickets, free downloads or anything that will help you attract followers. As to the type and quality of your engagement, this will depend on the number of 'followers' you attract and the level and depth of the relationships that you build.

(iv) Create good content

One of the best ways to attract and building a following on Facebook is to create good content. Today, people's attention span is very short, about eight seconds which is one second less than a goldfish! If you apply this to your posts, the first three to four words are critical if you are to get anyone's attention. The temptation for many people is to bare their soul on Facebook and on social media and write as much as possible. Too much text is not read on social media or at worse it is dismissed; because many people now view content on their mobile devices, which means posting lengthy text is likely to be ignored or even worse, deleted. Aim to create good, sharp, snappy content that's interesting and engaging, as this is the way to go, whether this is what you write, or the videos you post. Make your content relevant and remember getting people to view and engage with your content is what it is all about on Facebook and as Rome wasn't built in a day, so it will take time for you to create a following.

(v) Write snappy teasing headlines

Writing snappy, teasing and intriguing headlines to accompany your posts works on Facebook, as it does on all social media sites. Snappy headlines attracts people's attention, and if you directly ask them to 'share' your posts with their friends and followers, they are likely to do so and respond positively to you, especially if what you are proposing directly benefits others. Using correct grammar is also important as this will say a lot about you and your brand. Poor grammar will reflect badly on you as will poor photos and out-of-focus images.

(vi) Sharing photos

Creating content that people can share is at the heart of posting on Facebook and posting pictures is one of the best ways to do this. Photos are useful as they are 20 times more likely to get a reaction than mere text and they are likely to reach a wider audience. Posts pictures and images that are interesting, engaging and honest, for people have little time for dishonest posts. Your photos will say a lot about you, so avoid personal pictures and only post photos that are professional as these will show you and your music in the best light and help to draw people to your page. Where possible, posts pictures with other artists, especially those who are well-known in your field of music as these can help you get noticed and are an excellent way to attract followers.

(vii) Posting videos

Posting videos work even better than photos and images on Facebook and videos that are posted regularly, and have a good story to tell, are likely to attract comments. The more videos and moving images you post, the more likely it is you'll get a reaction, get people to engage with you, and if people like what you post, they are likely to share it with their friends and supporters. Take care however, not to fall into the trap of posting personal videos, images, footage or comments that have little or no relevance to your music. Remember, Facebook is a social platform, so make your posts interesting, aiming to spur, prompt or even provoke a reaction.

Your videos don't have to be full length. In fact, a series of 30-second video clips are much better and are likely to produce better results in attracting 'likes' and followers, than full-length ones. Clips that show you as an artist in situations with you and your music work well on Facebook. This means post videos of you rehearsing, 'before you go on stage', 'on the road', 'in the studio', 'with your fans', 'with other artists ' and virtually any situations to do with your music. It's the personal side of you as an artist that people will want to see and respond to, as it's their way of getting to know you, getting to know 'the person behind the music'.

(viii) Post good and interesting stories

Good photos attract comments on Facebook, as do exciting stories, especially if they are about you, your life and your music as an artist. People on Facebook like to read personal stories providing that they are honest and sincere. These posts get good reactions but be warned, people are quick to spot 'fake' or manufactured stories and are likely to react badly to them and turn away if they detect that what they are being fed is unreliable and untrue. Posts by themselves can be bland and uninteresting, so make yours interesting and engaging. You can do this by creating a buzz around what you post by using interesting photos, images and videos to help them stand out. Also, don't bombard your followers with dull, boring, irrelevant and uninteresting stories, as they will only switch off, leave your page and probably will never return.

(ix) Post regularly

There isn't any hard or fast rule on how often you should post on Facebook, although the site's analytics might suggest otherwise. Facebook has the technology to know how often a person posts, the time they spend on the site, how often people engage with your post and how your audience respond to what you've posted. This is Facebook's unique algorithm which ranks pages on the site according to a complex formula. As a rule of thumb, the more you routinely and consistently post, the more Facebook's algorithms will work to enhance and extend your posts, message and appeal. How often you should do this is a personal matter but remember that too many posts can be a turnoff, so aim to get the balance right. The received wisdom is that posts should be 'short and sweet', and that a person with fewer than 10,000 followers, should post once a day while those with a following of 10,000 or more, should post around once or twice a day.[24] The optimal times to post on Facebook to get the highest number of shares and clicks is Monday to Friday, anytime between 12 and 3 pm, and between 12 and 1pm at weekends. [25]

(x) Schedule your posts

Posting randomly and posting without a plan may not be the best way to post on Facebook. The best way to post is to have an idea on what you're going to post and when you intend to do this. Facebook can help you, as it has the facility (the analytics) to let you know the best time to post, and what posts works best for you. You can also use one of the automated scheduling websites like 'Hootsuite' and 'Promo Republic' to help you schedule your posts, and help you keep your followers informed and updated.

(xi) Leave comments and direct messages

Leaving a message or comment on Facebook page is another way to help build a following on the site. You should ask people to leave a message or comment and always remember to include a 'call to action' such as, 'leave a message' or 'let's begin a conversation,' as people are likely to respond to these type of requests. It's also worth noting that on social media, a 'call to action' works much better than posting 'worthy' Christian messages, useful though these may be.

(xii) Use Facebook reaction and emojis

Rather than just the option to'like,' Facebook now have emotional responses which anyone can use to signal their response to a post. These are emojis which have opened the way for people to react more precisely to what is posted. Many people, especially the young, now respond to posts by using emojis and they have become very popular, reducing the need to use words when an emoji will do.

(xiii) Advertising on Facebook works

Advertising works on social media including Facebook, otherwise, why would so many companies advertise on it. If your budget allows, you should advertise on the site as you can only do so much without money. By advertising, you'll begin to maximise your promotional opportunities and Facebook has some paid advertising packages to help you reach your target audience. These packages include driving people to your website, boosting your posts, offering 'greater reach for your campaigns', 'telling your brand's story, and 'increasing your engagements and sales.' Learn how they work and see if any of it is suitable for you.

(xiv) Facebook Live

'Facebook Live' once downloaded, is a new feature which allows live video streaming on the site. It's available on mobiles, iPads, iPhones and tablets and it is a great way for your followers to get close up and personal with you, and you to receive direct messages from your fans. 'Facebook Live' is also useful in many other ways. For example, if you have a new song coming out, you can let your fans/followers have a sneak 'live preview' of it before the public does. They can react to your broadcast with emojis and post their comments as you broadcast. 'Facebook Live' is a great way to help you build an audience and a following and a good way to help you deepen your relationship with your followers and fans. With 'Facebook Live' you can broadcast live from anywhere in the world spontaneously and the app even allows you also to do this as a monologue and your fans can post their comments as you speak, allowing you to respond to them. You should however let your followers know when you're going to broadcast so that they can tune in.

Some Simple Facts about Facebook

- Around 30 million people in the UK use Facebook, which is about half of the population.
- Around 45% uses the site regularly 'using it several times a day.
- Of those who use the Facebook, 84% are females compared to 73% males.
- The 23-37 age group uses the site more than any other age group and use it regularly.
- Photos are essential with over 300 million uploaded every day.
- Facebook has more active users than WhatsApp, Twitter and Instagram combined. [26]

Twitter

With over 500 million daily tweets and millions more tweeting every day on their mobile phones, it's easy to see why in a relatively short time, Twitter has become an important player in the world of social media and is a vital tool for any gospel artist wishing to build a following and promote their music. The site allows a user 280 characters to engage with, which keeps posts short and to the point.

The first thing to do on Twitter is to sign up to the site, and having done so, start to build a following. You should do this by making sure that your biography is entertaining and informative and that your profile picture is excellent, as these are the first two things anyone will see when they come across your page and this could decide whether they want to follow you or not, or retweet what you have posted/tweeted.

Targeting is essential on Twitter as it is on all social media and the more you target your tweets, the better your focus and the more success you're likely to have. You should first tweet people you know including your family, your friends, people in your church and people in the same line of business as you are. You can then widen this to include fellow musicians and other artists in your marketplace, as well as people whose music you are interested in and who are interested in your music.

Tweets which are personal and informal work well, but to get the best out of the site, you need to make sure that your tweets are relevant, and that they show your personality and give some idea of the person you are as an artist. Tweeting when you are in concert, when you're in a recording studio, when you are on the road, when you are writing songs, meeting fellow artists etc. are all useful tweets and providing they are relevant to your music and brand, they are likely to attract attention.

Use images with texts

Pictures and images work best on Twitter, especially moving images, and ever since the platform moved away from pure texting to allow videos, the number of people tweeting and engaging has increased tremendously. In fact, using images increases re-tweets manifold, and when you add photos, the engagement rate goes up quite a lot. Images create emotional bonds, and as a picture speaks a thousand words, so images and videos work best on Twitter and get more engagements.

Add videos

Adding videos works even better on the site and increases the level of engagement even more than photos. Videos last on the site for 140sec and most Twitter users watch videos that are on their timeline with some 82% of them being viewed on mobile devices. This means that you should make sure that your videos are capable of playing on mobile devices and that they are sharp, crisp and punchy, and able to hold a person's attention, because although 82% of Twitter users view videos on the site, 20% click away after just 10 seconds!

Use #Hashtags for they work

Twitter was the first to use hastags, the # without any spaces before a word. It's the way people now communicate online which makes tweets easy to follow and be followed. Today # is the vital sign used by nearly all social media sites which cause a word or phrase to become a searchable keyword. Hashtags mean that when you post a tweet, it is visible to both your followers and to anyone who shares an interest in what you have posted. Hashtags can be inserted anywhere in a post - the front, middle or at the end - and by choosing the right hashtag, you can reach a much wider audience with your posts as people now search and follow content by using specific hashtags.

Tweet in real time if possible

Today there are many tools for scheduling tweets, and although there's nothing wrong per se with automated tweets, people prefer and like real-time engagements, conversation and dialogue, rather than computerised tweets. It's best to tweet, closer to the weekend as Twitter traffic increases then, with Friday being the busiest. Spread your tweets out by at least 1 hour and tweet in the afternoon and preferably after 2 pm as Twitter traffic increases rapidly then.

Trending

A 'trend' on Twitter refers to a hashtag-driven topic which is popular at any given time on the site. It's not unusual for Twitter users to be tweeting about the same topic at the same time, and Twitter algorithms know the popularity and frequency of these topics or 'trends', by detecting a word or phrase that's used. With this information, the site lists the top 10 topics which are 'trending.' You can reach more people by adding your comments (tweet) to 'trending stories.'

Twitter Tips

1. Make sure that your profile is good and attractive with great photos and that there's a link to your website and all your social media accounts.

2. Tweet content that is valuable and interesting and that people will like to re-tweet. Remember to follow up all tweets and engage in real-time conversation for this works best.

3. Tweet frequently but not annoyingly. The more you tweet and interact with your followers the more they'll engage

with you, but strike the right balance between providing useful information and not annoying people with your tweets.

4. Show your personality in your tweets and avoid too many headlines, links and hashtags. Too many automated tweets annoy users as they can tell computerised tweets from the real ones.

Some Simple Facts about Twitter

*   Twitter has 13 million users in the UK
*   79 % of Twitter accounts are based outside of the USA
*   37 % Twitter users are between the ages of 18-29 and 25% between 30-49
*   80 % of Twitter users are on mobile [27]

12

Your Music and Social Media - 2

Instagram

Instagram is a mobile platform that allows anyone on the site to post photos and videos to users who are following them. By default, Instagram is a public platform, but it has a privacy function which anyone can activate. Pictures and moving images are the tool and lifeblood of this site and Instagram is an excellent tool for any gospel artist wishing to promote their music. It is one of the fastest growing social media network sites, and in just four years it has grown to over 200 million active monthly users, with an average of 70 million photos uploaded daily. The site is big on music, and despite being a photo app, four of its five most-followed accounts belong to music stars; Selena Gomez, Ariana Grande, Taylor Swift and Beyoncé. The site is very popular with young people, especially the 18-29 age group and with some site editing features, anyone can enhance their videos and pictures and make them more interesting, engaging and exciting to watch.

Build a following

Most artists from megastars to independent ones see Instagram as an excellent platform to promote their music and as a unique way to let their fans and followers know what they are doing. Like all social media sites, Instagram is all about attracting 'followers,' and building a following. This is what you should do if you want to be successful with your music on this site. To do this effectively, you will need to target what you post on Instagram as this will sharpen your focus and just like Facebook and Twitter, you should first target those in your nearest circle, inviting family, friends and those in your network to 'like' and 'follow,' you. Remember to insert a 'call to action,' inviting people to leave comments.

Making connections on Instagram

Making connections is essential to building an audience on Instagram and the more connections you make, the more Instagram's algorithms will respond to it by enlarging and extending your reach and following. What this means is that the more engagements or connections you can make, the more people will see what you have posted and the more Instagram's algorithms will respond to it. Your aim on Instagram is to connect and engage with as many followers as possible and you can do this by 'liking', replying and commenting on what is posted on the site.

When you post, make sure that your posts show up on your followers' feed as this is very important in building a following and how well you do this, will depend on the content of your post and the level of frequency. Posting music-based photos and images alongside photos that show you as a 'rounded' person works well on this site, as do photos and images that shows your identity and personality as an artist.

Remember that Instagram is a social media site, so join in the conversations, for its engagement and social interaction that will attract followers to you and your music.

Photos and videos work best on Instagram

When posting photos on Instagram make sure that they are fun, humorous and exciting as these attract attention rather than photos that are sombre or 'worthy,' as these can come across as dull and boring. Pictures evoke emotional and memorable responses in people and their effect can be long-lasting. Make sure that the photos you post are impressive as they can be powerful in attracting people to your music. Videos also work well on the site, and although you are only allowed 60-second videos, you can use this to your advantage by making short, sharp and snappy videos. Post videos like 'behind the scenes,' 'in the studio', 'in a recording session', 'in rehearsals', 'in concerts' etc as these are well-liked on the site and tend to positively influence people who view them. They work even better when posted as a sequence of short stories as they are likely to keep viewers interested as they anticipate, what's coming next.

Instagram Stories

Instagram has two relatively new features which are proving very popular and which you should think of using for your music. One is 'Instagram stories,' which is where a person posts a series of photos and video of their day in a 24-hour period which appears on the site as a slideshow. This last for 24 hours after which it is deleted. The advantage of 'Instagram Stories' is that they are discoverable not only by people who follow you but also by hashtags which means that many people can discover 'your stories,' if they are searching topics that they are interested in and it coincides with your 'story.' Instagram also allows live streaming and with this facility, you can now broadcast to people in real time and they in return can connect with you. Both facilities provide an excellent opportunity for you to attract new supporters to your music and if you use these services carefully, frequently and creatively, you'll find they are a great asset.

Instagram Tips

1. Sync Instagram to all your social media profiles including Facebook, Twitter, YouTube, etc.

2. Post behind the scene type photos and video clips including soundchecks, recording sessions, 'on the way to a gig', 'just before going on stage', 'in the dressing room' clips which not only show you as an artist, but also shows the human side of you, as people relate to this very much also on the site.

3. Post a series of photos over a couple of months rather than merely one-offs, for this will keep your supporters coming back for more as they anticipate what's coming next.

4. Use hashtags with photos and images, for this will group your pictures with other users on the site with similar photos and illustrations. The advantage is that it makes it easier for Instagram users to find you based on their interests and the hashtags they use.

5. Add captions and descriptions to your images and videos for this will contextualise your videos and pictures and help to explain them. Try to be brief, clear and to the point and don't forget to get your followers to share your photos and images with their friends and followers for this will help you build a following.

6. Reply and follow up every comment posted to you and always be gracious to those who have taken the trouble to comment on your pictures and posts. Let people know you appreciate their comments and support, for this will go a long way in helping you to build a support and fan base.

Some Simple Facts about Instagram

* There are 17.2 million users in the UK.
* 18-34 age group account for 61% of the user base
* Photos that feature faces get 32% more likes.
* 38% of Instagram Users are female with 26% male.
* The most popular hashtags on Instagram are: #Instagood #Loveme #Follow [28]

YouTube

YouTube is the second biggest social media site after Facebook and the most popular video-sharing site with over 3 billion users. 26% of these are in the UK (31million) with the 25-34 age group the most popular. YouTube is an excellent resource for any gospel artist wishing to promote their music, and an excellent tool for gaining followers (subscribers), building a brand and growing a fan base. As an artist, apart from uploading your music videos on the site, YouTube also allows you to have your own channel. You'll need to sign up for this and once you've done so, you should let your fans on your various other social media platforms know that you are on YouTube, and ask them to subscribe to your channel.

Being on YouTube is not merely about uploading your latest music video and seeing what happens, it's far more than that. It's about creating an attractive channel with exciting content that people will want to subscribe to and engage with, to learn about you, your music and your brand. Like any visual media, the more professional, creative, exciting and engaging your channel is, the more it is likely to attract followers.

Make use of the description box on the site

Now that you have created a YouTube Channel, the next stage is to write up information about you and your music in the description box. This is a useful and practical resource and if you use this properly, it can help to bring subscribers to your channel. Take care though with what you write, as your aim should be to draw viewers to your channel. Some professionals believe that you should use keywords and social media links as part of what you write, but it's best to research this to see what's best for you as both are equally good. The point here is to make good use of the description box, making sure that what you write is imaginative, exciting, compelling and unambiguous, encouraging people to engage with you and your channel. Don't underestimate what you write in the description box because YouTube uses the content to determine where it places your channel on its search page, increasing your channel's Search Engine Optimisation position.

Build a following

Like most social media sites, there are many ways to build a following on YouTube. Linking your YouTube channel to your other social media platforms is one way. Other ways are uploading videos regularly, commenting on other gospel artists' videos, asking people to comment and leave messages. These are all good ways of helping you to start building a following. Make sure your videos content is relevant and good as this will show that your channel is active, and with consistently good content, viewers/subscribers will come to look forward to what you post and seek out what's new on your channel.

Create an exciting Trailer

Creating an exciting and engaging promotional 'Trailer' will also help you build a following as it signals what your channel is about, what you are offering and the music people can come to expect of you. Embed a 'call to action' so that when people visit your channel, or view the videos, they can leave a message or a comment.

Post interesting videos

Merely posting music videos on YouTube is not enough to get viewers to subscribe to your channel. Viewers can see all the music videos they want, to so why should they go to your channel to watch your music videos? To get them to do this and engage with you, you'll need to target and have something interesting, enjoyable, exciting and even intriguing. Posting music videos alone is not enough, so post a mixture of videos including ones that are not music, as you're likely to attract a wide spectrum of subscribers, making people want to 'click' to view your channel. Post videos which are mysterious and which tempt visitors to click and view - it's the 'curiosity kills the cat' syndrome and remember to always add a 'call to action' for this will help to get comments, 'likes,'and 'shares'. YouTube algorithms will use these to decide where to rank your videos, and the higher your channel is listed, the more people will see your videos, and if they are using hashtags, the easier they'll be able to find you.

YouTube Channel is not about numbers but subscribers

Many people get overly impressed when they see new artists seemingly getting a lot of views on YouTube, not realising that although these views on the face of it is fine, what's far more important are the actual numbers of subscribers a channel receives. For example, a person searching for videos might come across one but barely spend a moment watching it. YouTube however record this as a 'view', even though that person might not like the video or want to engage with it.

A 'true view' is when a person clicks 'subscribe,' for by doing this, they are declaring an interest in the video and a person's channel, indicating a willingness to engage and by extension with the person whose channel it is. Subscribers are the real followers on YouTube, so don't get caught up with mere 'views', but don't underestimate them either!

Record a cover song, for they work on YouTube

Having a great song and great video is a no-brainer when it comes to attracting attention on YouTube or on social media generally, however with virtually hundreds of thousands of videos uploaded every minute, how is your song or music video going to stand out from the millions posted every day? One way is to record a cover song, preferably one that was once a hit, as you could be tapping into a latent army of supporters who know the song and could be open to your version. The trick is not merely to replicate the song but to give it a new treatment, a new lease of life, and to remain faithful to the original. Adding a great video will naturally help and will give you a head start, perhaps even bringing new subscribers to your channel.

Cover songs work on YouTube and there are many examples of artists who have found success and fame on the channel by doing this. There are thousands of well-known gospel songs to choose from and as part of your recording project you should record at least one or two of these. Covers are a ready-made path to potential success in the music business. One simple tip about posting a cover song on the site is that you should title your song similar to its original title. For example, if you were to record a cover of Kirk Franklin's hit song, 'Smile,' then you should title your version, something like: 'Kirk Franklin's Smile by X' (your name) or 'X (your name) sings, Kirk Franklin's Smile'. In this way, you are likely to pull in viewers attracted to the name 'Kirk Franklin' if they are searching using the hastag and also people who know the song 'Smile'!

Curated playlist can help to attract subscribers

Creating Playlists is another way to attract viewers and subscribers to your YouTube Channel. A Playlist is a list or group of videos that play one after the other on a channel, in the order that you have set. They are relevant because Playlists come up separately on YouTube search results increasing the number of times your channel is likely to be recognised. Make sure that you embed your Playlist on all your social media platforms, your website and blogs to increase awareness of both you, your music and your YouTube channel.

YouTube Tips

1. Try to upload videos consistently and where possible schedule this to get subscribers, as your fans and supporters will come to expect this. Consistent content will increase anticipation and participation, and will make your channel appear dynamic and professional.

2. YouTube has resources to help you increase subscribers and some inbuilt resources to help you grow your subscriber base. Research these and see what will work for you.

3. Use YouTube Analytics to know your audience and to know who is viewing your videos and a lot more besides. YouTube Analytics gives a range of beneficial information

such as who viewed your video, which part of the world or even part of the country they are from, and how long they spent watching it. YouTube Analytics will also help you know your audience and help you get a sense of what people think of the videos you post. It's knowledge like this which will help you tailor the videos and content of your channel so it reaches your target audience, rather than guessing what you think people might want or like.

Some Simple Facts about YouTube

- YouTube is the second largest search engine and third most visited website after Google and Facebook.
- More than half of YouTube views come from mobile devices.
- The 18-34-year age-group accounts for the most traffic distribution on YouTube.
- 80% of YouTube viewers are outside the USA
- On YouTube, 38% of users are female, and 62% are male.
- Users by age: 18-24 – 11%, 25-34 – 23%, 35-44 – 26%, 45-54 – 16%, 50-64 – 8%, 65+ – 3%, unknown age – 14%.[29]

Snapchat

Snapchat is a social media site that allows a person to take pictures and videos, add text to them and share them. Snapchat works by enabling users to send their photos, texts, images and videos to a controlled list of people called 'snaps' which disappears after 24 hours on the site. Today Snapchat is one of the fastest growing social media sites with over 160 million daily active users in the UK and over 400 million worldwide, 77% of which are students. It is a messaging app which only works on mobiles and it mainly appeals to young people. Like all social media sites, you need to build a following on

Snapchat to target your music to. One way to do this is to let your followers on all your other social media sites - Facebook, Twitter, YouTube etc - know that you are on Snapchat and ask them to follow you. If they are already on Snapchat, they're likely to be following you, anyway.

You should also use 'Snapchat Stories.' This is a relatively new feature and since its introduction it has become very popular. 'Snapchat Stories' allows users to put together a sequence of pictures, videos and images taken throughout a day and then add them to the 'My Story' facility on the site. 'Snapchat Stories' can then be viewed anytime and is stored sequentially in a 'chain' and lasts for 24 hours before it is deleted to make way for more videos and pictures. This process continues as long as the person who is posting wants to, which means, that 'My story' never really ends as it's always changing as a new sequence of 'stories' are posted which lasts for 24 hours before it too is replaced by a new sequence which lasts for 24 hours and is then deleted, and so on and so on.

The advantage of 'Snapchat Stories' is that as an ongoing sequence of events, it can help to create a bond between you who is posting the 'stories' and the recipient on the receiving end. These 'stories' are publicly available and as a consequence can potentially be seen by a large audience. Also as they are a continuous narrative, they tend to heighten people's expectation on what is coming next and help to draw people closer to what's been posted.

Snapchat appeals particularly to young people and 'Snapchat Stories' is a good way to build an audience for your music especially if you target it carefully. One idea is for a series of videos about your music over a 24-hour period making sure that what your post is interesting to share with an audience and your followers. If they are 'live' then all the better, as young people like 'live', 'rough and ready', 'on the spur of the moment', 'behind the scenes,' types videos as they work best as 'Snapchat Stories.' Make sure that they are humorous, intimate and engaging as dull, boring and uninteresting stories don't work. Don't be afraid to make your stories funny, quirky, spontaneous and even silly, and above all, be real with your 'stories', for this is what makes them work, and is the reason why the site is so popular with young people.

Snapchat Tips

1. Snaps appeals to the young: this is a site which young people like and they are not too worried about set up or stylised shots. They are more into the reality of what they are seeing or experiencing, so make your snaps fun, exciting and even quirky, for these are positives virtue on this site.

2. Keep your target audience in mind at all times: the more you know about the demographic of your target audience, the better and the more effective your snaps will be. Keep a clear idea of who your audience is, i.e. who is on the receiving end of your snaps, what are their interests, what type of music they like, where do they hang out and which artists do they like and are following. Research the market to know this for the more you know about your audience, the more you'll target your snaps efficiently.

3. Make compelling and memorable videos: photos and videos don't stay long on Snapchat so make sure that yours are memorable and exciting. Think always that the people on the receiving end of your snaps are your potential fans and make sure that your videos are good enough to grab their attention. Look at what you see successful artists are doing, and if what they are doing is working, adapt it to what you do, as they must be doing something right!

4. Create videos that give people an inside look: people on the site want to know about you not only as a gospel artist but also as a person. Post 'behind the scene' type videos for this will help you to introduce yourself and your music to potential followers. Use 'Snapchat Stories', features, individual lenses, filters, text and emojis, for these will enhance your videos and give people a more rounded picture of you and your music.

Some simple Facts about Snapchat

- Snapchat has around 100 million active daily users worldwide.
- About 30% of UK online users use Snapchat, with 16% using it daily.
- The site is very popular with females who account for about 34% of its total UK online population, with 25% being males.
- The main age group that uses the site is the 18-24 group who account for around 77% of all users.[30]

13

Pathway to Gospel Music Success

How to Succeed with your Music

There is an old Chinese proverb which says, *if you want to know the road ahead, ask those coming back.* Knowing the road ahead means avoiding the mistakes of the past, making sure not to repeat them, and looking forward to the future with hope and expectation. Digital technology, the internet and social media have opened the door wide for gospel music and today many people are walking through it to make their music. Speak to any gospel artist who's been in the business for any length of time, and they will tell you there's never been a better time to make gospel music in the UK, as anyone who wants to can now do so with very little effort. The application of technology to music production, the internet and social media have all helped in this process, plus the enormous growth in recent years of the Black Pentecostal church community. The problem every gospel artist now face, is how to make their music work for them and how to make it successful.

If you're a new gospel artist, you probably will need to discard all you've assumed about British gospel music, as the music has its own particular way of behaving and operating. For example, there's a general assumption in the music business that being 'different' creatively, is a good thing. On the surface that's probably true, but in gospel music this can have the opposite effect. Being 'different' in gospel can mean being 'worldly', 'ungodly' even, and as such, mean failing to be recognised or at worse, being dismissed. In gospel music, being familiar in sound, style and music is often reassuring and indicates not straying from the faith so in this sense being 'different' might not be a good thing. Being 'different' can also be construed as coded language for being 'secular' which is the last thing any gospel artist would want to be seen as or have implied about their music. Being 'different' in gospel music should mean that your music is better than the competition, you have better songs, better sound, better production, better vocals and that your performance is better than most. This will help you, help your music become known and help it stand out in the market place. It is knowing the path to take with your music which is important, and below are a few suggestions to help you.

Have a Consistent Visual Identity and Style

Maintaining a consistent style in all aspect of your music project is essential if you are to succeed with it. This mean that all your graphics and artwork, whether it's your CD design, your social media sites, your website, your printed materials, blogs, newsletters etc or any of your electronic images, should all have a similar style look, feel and design. They will reinforce each other becoming one visual output consistent with your identity and brand.

Songs are Everything

As a gospel artist it's natural that you will want to write your own songs, and while this is entirely understandable, it's unlikely that you'll have the ability or experience to write good songs. Naturally, there are exceptions, but writing 'good songs' calls for a great deal of craft, skill, experience and ability and this doesn't happen overnight. As a new artist what you should do before attempting to write your own songs is to spend some time researching songs, both past and present, unpicking them to see how they are 'made' and how they are put together. The songs are everything and it is this which will make your album/EP work - that's the bottom line! Good production, great vocals will all help but the songs are EVERYTHING, and it is the songs that will draw people to your music, make people remember you and make your music successful. Your songs will define you as an artist, and if you're a new artist or even an established one, you will need good songs – no, great songs if you're going to succeed with your music!

Most songs are 'constructed' – they are made, and that's why they are 'good songs' and we remember them. Hit songs are songs that are cleverly written and crafted and that's why they are hits. This mean that if you want to be successful with your music, you will need good songs, although this is easier said than done. Gospel cover songs can help you and you should research them as this is a good way to start, rather than rushing to record the first songs that come into your head or what you think you've been inspired to write, when your song writing ability has never been tested.

As part of your research, you should deconstruct songs to see how they are made and how they are put together. The more you know how this is done, the more this knowledge will subtly influence your own writing, and subconsciously feed into your creativity. Most gospel songs tend to follow a format: intro, verse, chorus, verse, chorus, bridge, chorus, outro. The Intro is the start of the song which tries to capture the listener's attention. The verse tells the story of the song and depending on the story there may be many verses. The Chorus is usually the central part of a song and the part which most people remembers. It's often the 'payoff' of the story in the song and that's why it's repeated several times. The 'musical bridge', on the other hand is what it says it is - a bridge to get the song from one part to another. The bridge also adds variety to a song and help to make it enjoyable, rather than it being dull boring and repetitive. Musicians have a number of tricks to help them do this, with chord progression being one of many ways.

Always Get a Second Opinion on Your Songs

If you do decide to write your own songs, you should get a second, independent, honest opinion and assessment. It's best to get someone in the same line of music as you are and avoid family and friends, (unless they can be relied on to be independent), as they are likely to say what they think you want to hear, rather than give an objective assessment. Learn from the criticisms you get about your songs as they can be useful, and if your song needs restructuring and the lyrics need rewriting, then that is what you should do, as it's normal for a song to go through many changes before it's ready to be recorded. Remember that if a friend or colleague writes the lyrics to your songs or has helped and collaborated with you on them, that both of you should agree what each has done and write this up in a simple letter of agreement, stating in percentage terms how each of the song should be divided between you. Do this before you record, as it's likely to save you a great deal of time and possibly even money, if there is ever a falling out and it is disputed who did what on a particular song.

Make Your CD Look Great

Although this is changing, graphically most UK gospel CDs leave a lot to be desired. It's difficult to call to mind any recent gospel album or sleeve (maybe one or two) that are outstanding and memorable. There are countless examples in other forms of music but not as many in British gospel music. A well-designed CD is a strategic marketing tool which you shouldn't ignore, and if you do, you do so at your peril. Your CD is likely to be the first thing that a person sees and is likely to be what you are judged by and, by implication, your music. How your CD looks can play a big part on how you and your music are perceived, and could well determine how people react and respond to you. A well-designed CD is likely to attract people's attention and immediately this will give you a head start over your competitors. Excellent graphics will get you noticed, will set you apart as an artist, and if your known for producing good graphics, subconsciously people will be attracted to your music.

Sell Your CD From Your Website - sell digital downloads from music sites

Apart from your website where people can get information about you and your music, your site should also be the only place where people can buy the physical copy of your CD. You'll get a much better return if you sell the physical copies on your website rather than if you were to sell them on music websites, which tend to discount heavily, anywhere between 15 and 30%, leaving you with little profit. Selling your CDs from your website can also mean capturing email mail addresses which is a vital tool in your armoury. It can also mean driving traffic to your website and is a good way to build support for your music. However, a note of caution. When anyone buys from your site, make sure that you treat them with the utmost care, courtesy and respect. Make sure that every purchase is dispatched quickly, possibly within two days maximum, and if for any reason there is a problem and a customer complains, always believe the customer and reimburse them for any purchase or offer a replacement. Try to keep your customers satisfied, for if they are happy, they're likely to talk about it and share their experience with their family and friends. If, on the other hand, they've had a bad experience, they are likely to let the whole world know!

You Will Need PR

Most independent artists including gospel ones often underestimate the importance of PR (public relations) in the promotion of their music. Most gospel artists put PR low on their list of priorities, mainly because they don't really understand it, and even when they do, they are not convinced of its efficacy and think that it is too costly for what they think they'll get in return. What PR does for your music is to communicate it to the media and to your target audience. As an artist, any PR you do, whether you buy it in or you do it yourself, it should first be about raising your profile and raising awareness of your music. It's not about looking at ways to get people to buy your CDs as there's no proven correlation between what PR does and CD sales. This is a wrong way of looking at PR. PR uses marketing and promotional tools to get publicity for your music, essentially making the media aware of it and they in return tells everybody. It's often a chicken and egg situation. You need promotion to get your music known, and it is by publicising your music, that it becomes known. What a PR expert can do is bring your music to the attention of the media and the public. In your case as a new gospel artist, not the whole world or even the entire Christian market, but specifically, to people in your market place or who are interested in your type of music - your target audience. The more experienced your PR person is on your target market, the more effective they'll be in publicising your music.

You Will Need a Press Kit or EPK

Most artists who have a record deal will have a press kit as part of the publicity for their music. A press kit is usually a brochure which sets out all the essential information about an artist, including their biography, CD, press cuttings and a few well-chosen photographs. In the music business, there are two types of Press Kit, one printed and the other an electronic version, commonly known as an EPK (electronic press kit). Both contain the same information; with the EPK, the artist's music is likely to be in the form of an MP3 or a Wave file, while in the printed copy, the music is usually the physical copy of an artist's CD. Most EPKs today are downloadable PDFs which people now get from artists' websites.

There is no right or wrong way to produce a Press Kit, and if you are considering one, think of an electronic one, for a brochure press kit is likely to be expensive. At a minimum, your EPK should have your biographical details, two good photos, any press reviews and an MP3 of your music. The biographical information should give a good overview of who you are as an artist, including your influences, aspiration and development. You should make sure that what you write is informative, exciting and succinct, and remember that the intention is to offer a good overview rather than your life story. State what your aims are as a gospel artist, avoid religious clichés, and if you use religious or Christian terms, 'I want my music to touch souls' etc, explain what you mean by this in everyday language. Photos are important, and you should make sure they are high resolution at least 300 dpi (dots pixels per inch), preferably taken by a professional photographer and converted to a jpg or tif file.

Whether the photos are in colour or black and white doesn't matter, for what's important is that the quality is good and that they are well shot. Where possible, avoid pictures of you in stereotypical 'Christian settings' - doves all over the place, a garden of Eden-type backdrop, waterfalls, clouds, sunsets - as they are clichéd and have been done a thousand times. Be careful also not to replicate urban stereotypical street images so beloved of Rap artists, as they too are clichéd and boring. Steer clear as well of exotic locations that bear no resemblance to you as an independent gospel artist, as you're fooling no one. Seeing you in exotic locations that bear no resemblance to your status as a gospel artist won't help your music, for it makes you appear pretentious nor is it prophetic, it's just simply silly. What you should aim for is that all visual portrayals of you and your music are honest, have visual integrity and that they compliments your music and are not at variance with it.

Your CD recording or MP3 is an essential part of both your EPK and press kit for it will say more about you than anything that's written. You should make sure that your CD is professionally recorded, mixed and mastered. You should also include a 'radio edit' of the single or lead track, for this is what radio DJs and presenters will look for to play or to review when they want to play your music. Remember to make your EPK the best that it can be, because this is what DJs, music journalists, reviewers and people in the business use to get information about you. It is also what PR specialists use to send out information to the media about your music.

Finally, remember that your music is everything and no matter how good your press kit is, how well it is designed, or how well it's written, if your music isn't up to scratch or isn't good enough, no amount of a press kit will help you! Your music is everything, and this is what you should concentrate on as this is what ultimately you'll be judged on. Remember also to include all your contact details on your EPK - which many people forget to do- so that people can easily reach you.

Learn From People Who Are Better Than You

One way to improve on what you do as a gospel artist, is to watch what other gospel artists are doing well. Study them carefully and learn how for example, they structure their songs, what type of songs they sing especially the ones that are popular, how they put their music together and if they do live shows, study their performances and learn how they stage their shows and concerts. Never stop learning and developing your music and if you see an artist doing something well, learn from that artist. There is always something to learn, and if you want to get ahead and stand out with your music, you should always be prepared to learn. It is by learning, growing and developing your music that your artistry will improve and the more you learn and the more work you put into your music, the more confident you'll become. It's at this level of work and ability that your confidence will grow and you'll come to understand gospel music at a deeper level which will help to fuel your creativity and in turn, help you find your own sound and identity.

Practising every day is vital; in fact, spending something like 80% of your time on your music is about the right proportion if you are serious and want to be successful. You will need to live, sleep and breathe gospel music almost to the point of obsession if you want to be successful, and it's only when your mind is full of gospel music and is transformed by it, that you'll be able to pour it out as a creative offering. Remember to spend time also on the business side of your music - don't neglect this but give it equal weight as you should with all other aspect of your music. Above all, remember that it's your music that counts, and it is this what people will judge you by and what will bring people to you.

Work to Your Strengths and on Your Weaknesses

Apart from acquiring several skills you'll need for your music, there are other qualities that it's worth having too. For example, every artist has their strengths and weaknesses, and it's by working TO your strength and ON your weaknesses that you are likely to grow and develop as an artist. No one would call Kirk Franklin the world's greatest singer, but no one in gospel music is better with an audience, is more original, is a better front man or can write better songs than Kirk. What Kirk lacks in his singing ability, he compensates for by using the best singers on his records and for his live performances. Like any good artist, Kirk plays to his strengths and because of this he has developed a style that is uniquely his. Not every gospel artist can be a great singer, writer or musician, but everyone can improve on what they have and it's constant practice that brings improvement.

Church Ministry

Most of the live work you're likely to get as a new gospel artist will almost certainly be in churches rather than in gospel concerts. If this comes to you and you are invited to a church to minister/perform, you should take this very seriously and look at it as a great opportunity. Pastors in British gospel music are very influential, and if a pastor, especially those with large churches, get behind your music and decide to support you, it can make all the difference to you and your music. Pastors are the best salespersons you can ever want, and if you have a long-term relationship with a pastor, it can mean constant work for you, and an excellent source of data for your mailing list, as well as a ready-made market for your CDs and a good source of revenue. Don't look at this lightly and you must be organised and ready to take advantage of this when it comes.

When you are invited to perform/minister at a church, you should first agree with the pastor on the essential terms of your ministry/ performance. Don't get too hung up about payment at this stage and see playing as an opportunity for your music and a chance to sell your CDs. As soon as you are able, contact the church engineer to make sure that the church PA system, microphones and monitors are suitable for your performance. If possible, you should visit the church beforehand to get a feel of the place and speak to the pastor or preferably the music minister to find out the songs that are popular in the church. When it comes to putting your 'set' (the songs you are going to sing) together, be sure to include a couple of the songs that are sung in the church.

Unless you're given a specific length of time, keep your set short and sweet, perhaps three songs unless the pastor asks for more. Your first song should be a well-known one that the congregation knows and can join in with you on, for this will help to break the ice and quickly get the congregation on your side. The second song can be your own song or your current single but before singing it, plug your CD, your website and your social media sites. Most pastors won't mind you doing this but make sure that you do this tactfully and tastefully, avoiding any hard sell. In fact, as a matter of courtesy, and as part of your promotions, offer your CDs at a special reduced price of 50%, both to encourage sales and as a thank-you to the pastor and church for inviting you. Your third song should either be another that the church knows or one of your own - but preferably one that the church knows.

Without a Sound Check, You Perform at Your Own Risk

Whenever you perform or minister, you will need a sound check, and without one, you are risking your music and your reputation. A sound check is very important, and the first thing you should do when invited to a church or concert hall is to find out who the engineer is and make contact to discuss your sound check and your performance. It's possible that as a new artist you'll be using 'backing tracks'; let the engineer know this and if you have a 'technical rider' (Sound and PA specifications), send this along with your EPK (electronic press kit) so that the engineer has as much information about you and your music as possible.

A Sound Check is what it says it is. It's the time allocated to check your sound and the technical requirements for your performance. It is not a time to rehearse or a time to run through your set as you should have done this already during your own rehearsals. How long you will need for your sound check will depend on the time that's been allocated to you or what you've negotiated with the engineer or pastor. Make sure that you and the engineer are both clear on the time and duration of your sound check to avoid any disappointment when you turn up for a sound check only to find there's no time left, with all the potential pitfalls that this entails.

Your soundcheck matters and it is the vital ingredient that is likely to make your concert/ministry work and your performance memorable. From an audience point of view, there's never any excuse for a poor or a bad sound in a concert or at a church ministry. If the sound is bad, this is what people are likely to remember, and if they had to pay to hear you, they'll never forget and will feel doubly cheated. Always cooperate with the sound engineer, because an engineer can make you sound good by working to get the best sound for you, or the reverse if you have rubbed the engineer up the wrong way. You cannot afford to take this risk or risk your sound as with today's social media, people are all too keen to post their reviews of your performance on line for the whole world to know.

Performing Live

When you are asked to perform with a band, you shouldn't take this lightly either, for this can be the difference between your music taking off or you experiencing a setback with it. Playing in front of an audience is both an art and a craft and while every performance is different, and every artist performs in their own way, playing live is what every artist should strive to do - sharing their music with an audience and the audience in return having a pleasant and an enjoyable experience. Make sure that you have thoroughly rehearsed what you're going to perform so that your performance is professional, your music is tight and you appear as a serious artist. You should practise your 'set' from start to finish, including all that you'll say between the songs. This also mean making sure your band and singers know what they are doing not only on every song but also if you've incorporated any moves in your performance. You should aim to make your performance as an integrated musical experience that both enhance your songs and create a good experience for your audience. Don't try to wing your performance, for this hardly ever works and you're not experienced enough; even experienced artists don't take this risk with their performances.

Don't preach either when you're asked to perform, as this can be very off-putting and will disappoint your audience. People go to gospel concerts because they want to see an artist perform, be entertained as well as spiritually uplifted. It's no good throwing some songs together either, and wrapping them up in spirituality and offer them to your audience. They won't be impressed, and as gospel audiences are generally musically savvy, they'll see through what you are doing and won't be impressed.

As a gospel artist, every time that you perform, whether it's in a concert hall, a church or anywhere, try to ensure that your audience have a good experience and that they take something away with them from your performance. If you need to link your songs, you should rehearse what you are going to say beforehand and integrate it with your performance. Avoid being trite and keep your comments short, sweet and to the point, remembering that you are not on stage to instruct or preach, but to share your songs and offer them as a spiritual offering, both to God and to the audience that has come to see you. Don't forget your music is gospel and that it has a long and venerable history. Your audience is likely to have high expectations, so be careful not to disappoint.

Church Service or Gospel Show?

There's a constant tension in gospel music between people happy to see gospel concerts as partly a 'show,' and those who are opposed to this view, believing a gospel concert can never be such, as it is an act of worship. It's neither one nor the other, but both. What is a 'show' other than in the strict sense, an opportunity to display, exhibit, expose, view or to reveal; and to suggest that gospel concerts shouldn't be any of these is simply folly. In general, people go to gospel concerts because they want to see an artist live and want to experience their music. Gospel audiences do not differ from any other audiences in this regard and will expect all the paraphernalia associated with a good concert, i.e. sound, stage, lighting, etc. Where the difference lies is that gospel audiences, apart from expecting a 'show', expect a spiritual experience from a gospel concert as well! It's a gospel artist's ability to strike the right balance between the two, that will mark them out as a great performer.

If You Can't Get Church Ministry, Look Elsewhere

It's difficult to get into churches if you are an unknown artist and if this is you, you should look elsewhere for other opportunities to showcase your music. This may be at your local youth club, wine bar, conferences, gatherings, weddings, christenings, birthday parties, banquets, shows, or even funerals. In fact, you should take any opportuntiy, anywhere where you can find an opening for your music, and not wait for the 'big one', getting into a church or on a concert stage. You should look at these opportunities as part of your apprenticeship, for the more experience you have and the more different audiences you play to, the better you'll become, the more professional you'll be and the tighter will be your music and performance.

Think Outside the Box

The traditional model for most gospel artists is to make a CD, sell enough of it, get plenty of concerts and ministry bookings and become well known. For a few gospel artists this works but for most this won't happen; but there are other ways you can make a success of your music. You should 'think outside the box,' i.e. look at new and creative ways of making your music work for you. For example, today there are gospel artists who although they started out on a traditional road with their music, have since gone in a complete and different direction. For example, some now see their music as an outreach and now take their music into old people's homes, prisons, mental institutions, schools and into local community organisations. Others are partnering with local agencies and charities such as Help the Aged, Christian Aid, Tearfund, Compassion etc.

in a creative relationship where both the artist and the charity benefits. Some also run music projects in schools teaching children how to sing gospel music, as well as helping them to build their confidence and self-esteem. Others have found green pastures abroad in Europe, staging gospel music master classes, concerts and music workshops.

The lesson here is don't get stuck in thinking that being a gospel artist only means recording a CD and waiting on invitations to perform in churches and in concerts. There are so many other ways for you to get your music and ministry known and you should take advantage of these. You could also explore forming a relationship with local businesses and community organisations where you offer your music in a strategic partnerships by adding value to what local companies and community organisations are doing. You could always offer to play an acoustic set for free at your local business and community events on the basis that you can sell your CDs. You may not sell buckets of CDs but you will gain valuable experience playing to different audiences, plus gain a great deal of goodwill and contacts for your music. Remember, you can always add value with your music to what people are already doing, which means looking at your music in a multi-dimensional way which is the way music is generally now going anyway.

Stage Your Own Concerts

Staging your own concerts is an excellent way to grow your music, as the more practice you have at performing live, the more you will develop a unique sound and style. Performing 'in concert' is always a good place to show your talent, but getting live concert bookings is hard to come by in British gospel. You could stage your own concert, but this is very risky and costly and you could lose a lot of money so make sure you have a big following and good fan base.

'The Humblest Cow Sucks the Most Milk'

This is a Caribbean saying – even a Jamaican one - that the more humble and easy going you are as a person, the more people will be willing to help you. In other words, as well as having the necessary skills and expertise as a gospel artist, if you are to succeed with your music, you are going to need other attributes as well. Qualities such as humility, patience, honesty and flexibility will get you everywhere. These are Christian virtues which you should have if you are going to make an impression and have any effect with your music. It's no good being arrogant, big-headed and inflexible, for this will only get people's backs up, give you a bad name and a bad reputation which you might find hard to shake off. Co-operating, offering to do what other artists choose not to do, being modest and helpful, are all excellent Christian qualities. Develop them, and they will attract people to you and your music and open doors for you.

APPENDICES

References

1. Cavendish, R, (6th June 1998), 'Arrival of SS Empire Windrush', *History Today*, Vol 48

2. Glennie, A, Campell L (16th June 2010), *Migration Policy Institute*

3. Forces War Records: Unit History, British West Indian Regiment: https://www.forces-war-records.co.uk/ units/134/british-west-indies-regiment

4. BBC News: 'Soldiers of the Caribbean: Britain's forgotten war heroes', Claire Brennan, 13th May 2015: www.bbc.co.uk/news/uk-32703753

5. *Just a Little While*, E M Bartlett (1885-1941)

6. The Doxology - *Praise God from Whom all Blessings Flows*, Thomas Ken (1637-1711) https://hymnary.org/text/ praise_god_from_whom_all_blessings_ken)

7. Edwards, Joel (ed.) (1992) *Let's Praise Him Again: An African Caribbean Perspective on Worship*, Kingsway Publication Eastbourne.

8. Sampson, Cheryl A. (January 2015), 'Hymn Lining: A Black Church Tradition with Roots in Europe', *The Spectrum: A Scholar's Day Journal*, Vol 3, Article 9

9. The Billy Graham Library, Crusade City Spotlight: London, August 3 2012
https://billygrahamlibrary.org/crusade-city-spotlight-london/

10. ibid

11. Review: Across the Bridge/Where Shall I Go, Cross Rhythm, Mike Rimmer, 1ˢᵗ January 2009
http://www.crossrhythms.co.uk/products/SoulSeekers/Across_The_BridgeWhere_Could_I_Go/49848/

12. *Where Do I Go From Here?* Jim Reeves (1923 -1964), from the Album, *We Thank Thee*.

13. *When God Dips His Love in My Heart* Tennessee Ernie Ford (Cleavant Derricks 1910-1977), *40 Treasured Hymns*

14. A History of Hymns, 'Precious Lord, Take My Hand, Printed in *Discipleship Ministries,* C Michael Hawn

15. ibid

16. Mahalia Jackson, The Queen of Gospel (1947-56)
www.mahaliajackson.us/biography1947.php

17. Crittendon, David (6ᵗʰ August2015), 'Reverend James Cleveland, King of Gospel, *The Neighbourhood News Online*

18. www.officialcharts.com/artist/22195/inspirational-choir

19. Walters, Darren (2009), 'Nepstar, 10 Years of Change', BBC News

20. Broughton, Viv (1996), *Too Close to Heaven: Illustrated History of Gospel Music*, Midnight Books

21. Turner, Steve (2010), *An Illustrated History of Gospel*, Lion Hudson Plc

22. Smith, Steve Alexander, Robinson, Noel (2009), *British Black Gospel: The Foundations of This Vibrant UK Sound*, Monarch Books

23. Meade, Bazil (2011), *A Boy, A Journey, A Dream: The Story of Bazil Meade and The London Community Gospel Choir*, Monarch Books

24. Social Report Blog, 3rd May 2018, 'How Often Should You Post On Social Media?' https://www.socialreport.com/insights/article/115003574046-

25. www.hootsuite.com

26. The Latest Social Media Statistics 2018, Allison Batisby: www.avocadosocial.com

27. Twitter by Numbers stats. Demographics. Omicoreagency.com

28. Social Media Technology: www.nilssmith.com/blog/15-interesting-facts-about-instagram

29. Mind Blowing YouTube Facts, Figures and Statistics 2018: www.merchdope.com/youtube-statistics/

30. Snapchat: www.nilssmith.com/blog/10-interesting-facts-about-snapchat

Song List

HYMNS AND GOSPEL SONGS

Below are the songs I've quoted in the first section of this book. I encourage you to go online and listen to them as many are classic and illustrate some of the themes I've covered.

Soon This Life Will All Be Over

https://youtu.be/33x0G4Q3XL0

Praise God, From Whom All Blessings Flow

https://youtu.be/DnsAofIMHIw

A brilliant version of this song which I only came across while writing this book. It's by the Roberta Martin Singers - James Cleveland mentor Roberta Martin is a gospel singer in her own right.

West Indians sing this song but not as slow. This is a wonderful version.

https://youtu.be/YYtG3YKv26E

This is more how West Indians sing this doxology

There Were Ninety and Nine

https://youtu.be/pXg0p0imY_A

There are many versions of this song online, with the Gaithers' rendition a very good example of the beauty of this song.

Oh Happy Day That Fixed My Choice

https://youtu.be/Tn7ZCh_Qjow

This is a good indication of how 'Oh Happy Day' sounded before Edwin Hawkins turned it and arranged it into the phenomenal gospel song it became. Sometimes the song segues into 'On Jorden Stormy Banks', another great gospel number.

Oh Happy Day - Edwin Hawkins Singers

https://youtu.be/TrjLRvkYTqc

The original recording of this iconic gospel number with the Edwin Hawkins Singers

Billy Graham - 'Just as I am, without one plea.'

https://youtu.be/NlYUAM5YoNU

Author: Charlotte Elliott

Tune: Woodworth

Billy Graham Crusades - Harringay Arena & Earls Court

https://youtu.be/Fx_Tsc9IheM

https://youtu.be/F2fGZ2JNAeI

Cliff Richard - What Friend We Have in Jesus

https://youtu.be/dgjBWw0zfEk

Billy Graham at Wembley Stadium

https://youtu.be/XWO6e29qtq8

How Great Thou Art

https://youtu.be/XlfcvUtUoOM

Not many people know that the 'King of Rock n Roll', Elvis Presley was a gospel singer and that is singing was steeped in the genre. In this powerful rendition Elvis shows this clearly.

Carrie Underwood gives an equally great modern performance of this number

https://youtu.be/XlfcvUtUoOM)

Author: Carl Gustav Boberg

CHARLES A TINDLEY

Nothing Between

https://youtu.be/8Y9JXPbzONc

By and By

https://youtu.be/MwhgR-yvNI4

Leave It There - Take Your Burden to the Lord

https://youtu.be/1t5lkZ4YIeY

Stand By Me

https://youtu.be/khDb3kbErTQ

The Storm is Passing Over

https://youtu.be/d3jgPsGQSdQ

THOMAS DORSEY

Precious Lord, Take My Hand

https://youtu.be/kA0UV62zQFc

This wonderful performance is by the man himself, Thomas A Dorsey, taken from the best documentary on gospel music, 'Say Amen Somebody' by George T Nierenberg

It's A High Way To Heaven

https://youtu.be/LhWNU7QRwS4

MAHALIA JACKSON

Mahalia at the Newport Jazz Festival 1958

https://youtu.be/06gAdro-62E

Move On Up a Little Higher

https://youtu.be/06gAdro-62E

In the Upper Room

https://youtu.be/OLZcoDsPUkI

Mahalia Jackson @ Newport Jazz Festival 1958

https://youtu.be/rq7Kf25Dou0

JIM REEVES

We Thank Three

https://youtu.be/qwZUszJmZyc

This is Jim Reeves' Classic gospel album so beloved of West Indians during the 1960s. It contains many songs sung in West Indians homes and churches, including the track 'Where Do I Go From Here.'

Producer: Chet Atkins

RCA Victor-CD RCA (WM) 6008

TENNESSEE ERNIE FORD

Amazing Grace - 40 Treasured Hymns:

https://youtu.be/HiCkKvYoUAE

Audio CD (November 8, 2012)

Number of Discs: 2

Format: Dual Disc

Label: Sunset Productions

ASIN: B00A44I5M2

JAMES CLEVELAND
Peace Be Still & The Angelic Choir - Savoy Records -1963
https://youtu.be/yfIjj-wN93Y

ARETHA FRANKLIN
What a Friend We Have in Jesus
-Amazing Grace Album-1972
https://youtu.be/z9rrtgwRsfk
Amazing Grace-1972
https://youtu.be/jIBqCVWjqV8
Atlantic Records
Producers: Jerry Wexler, Arif Mardin, Aretha Franklin

ANDRAE CROUCH
Take Me Back
https://youtu.be/a0I9iEUfRvI
Oh It Is Jesus - Light Records
https://youtu.be/pn12xo2Dwas

THE WINANS
Count it All Joy
https://youtu.be/T0RiyYbs5Ro
Question Is
https://youtu.be/05KfzUl6OYY

Glossary

13th Amendment, 1865
This Amendment to the American Constitution effectively legally abolished 'slavery and involuntary servitude'.

Acapella Singing
Unaccompanied singing, without instruments

Accept Christ as a Personal Saviour
A person in a Pentecostal church choosing to commit to becoming a Christian.

Altar Call
This is the part in a Pentecostal Church Service when a person is invited to commit their life to Christ. They usually show this by going to the Altar at the front of a church where they are prayed for. This act signifies that they've become a Christian and is then accepted as part of the broader Christian community.

Backing Tracks
This is recorded music to which a soloist sings to, or a musician plays along to - the recorded music without the vocals.

Billy Graham Crusade
These were the meetings or church services Billy Graham conducted all over the world. They were called Crusade because Billy Graham saw his mission as fighting against sin/

evil/wickedness/darkness and by doing this bringing people to Christ - the light of the world!

Born Again

This is Pentecostal speak for becoming a Christian, which is a deliberate act of will in which a person agrees to 'accept Christ as a Personal Saviour' and agrees to live by and follow His teaching.

Bringing the Word/Delivering the Message

A sermon-call on to preach.

Call and Response

Call and Response is what it says - one musical phrase (call) is followed by another (the response). This is a tradition that began in slavery and was a feature of the songs that slaves sang as they worked. Today "Call and Response" is expressed in many ways - in religious gatherings, Western church music (Antiphony), Pentecostal services ('can I get an Amen?'), sports gatherings and in a multiple of music forms -in gospel, blues, jazz, R&B and hip-hop.

Call to Be Saved

The same as accepting Christ as a personal saviour.

Campground Meetings

These were secret meeting usually some distance from the slave master's house where the slaves would meet to sing, dance and shout in their own African way. They sang and dance to ease the pain of their enslavement and to hope for a time when they would be free. The slave would 'ring shout' where they would gather in a circle, and sing, shout, clap their hands, dance and chant ecstatically often ending up in a trance. The singing from these campground meetings was the precursor of the 'Spirituals.'

Civil Rights Movement
This was a movement in America during the 1950s and 60s when Black people fought for social justice and for Black people to be treated equally in American society. The springboard was Rosa Parks - a Black woman who refused to give up her seat to a white man at the front of a bus she was travelling in as the segregation laws of Alabama dictated. Rosa Parks was arrested and a young Baptist Minister - Martin Luther King - was asked to lead a boycott of the bus company.. This incident ignited the Civil Rights Movement, the general struggle for equality and justice under the law for Black people in America.

Colour Bar
An unofficial social system that existed in some parts of Britain in the 1960s when Blacks and Asians were 'barred' from certain places.

Copyright
This is the legal right in the case of music that protects the use of a song or sound recording. Copyright law governs the rules on how the songs and recordings can be used. For a work (song) recording to be copyrighted, it needs to be an 'original' product of a person's skill and intellectual property' as well as being 'tangible' which means the song or recording needs to be expressed in a physical format. Record, digital download, streaming etc.

Cover Song
This is a new recording or a performance of a song by an artist other than by the original that was once commercially released.

Devil's Music

The blues historically in America is known as 'devil's music' mainly because of its long association with the lifestyle and music of a section of Black America during the 1900s with the establishment of Ragtime (the forerunner of jazz), Barrelhouse music, Juke joints (clubs), Speakeasies (illegal drinking club during prohibition) and Creep joints (brothels). As far back as 1800, the word 'blue' was slang for being drunk and therefore the religious part of Black America disapproved of music coming out of these places calling it 'devil's music.'

Devotional Service

In West Indian churches this refers to the first part of the service - the more formal part. It's usually characterised by a hymn, prayer and scripture reading.

Digital Technology

Digital technology is the process that enables a large quantity of information to be compressed, delivered at speed and stored on mobile phones, computers, laptops, and other such devices. It describes the electronic technology that generates, stores, and processes data.

Diocese

Diocese is a district or parish under the pastoral care of a bishop in the Christian Church.

Doxology

Doxology is an expression of praise to God in Christian worship. In West Indian Pentecostal churches this signals the end of the service and is often the final song before the benediction - the blessing. A typical doxology in West church services is 'Praise God from whom all blessings flow, praise Him all creatures here below, praise, praise Him above the heaven and the earth, praise father son and holy ghost - Amen.' In contemporary Christianity, 'Gloria Excelsis' is a well-known doxology.

Emancipation Proclamation 1863
This was the declaration issued by President Lincoln that 'all persons held as slaves within any State or designated part of a State...shall be then and forever free.' This did not in itself abolish slavery - that came with the 13th Amendment.

Empire Windrush
The SS Empire Windrush was a former German cruise ship that was used to transport the first batch of West Indians to Britain to help in the reconstruction of the country after World War II.

Enoch Powell (1921-1998)
Enoch Powell was an influential British Conservative politician and a former Minister of Health and Shadow Defence Secretary. On April 20th, 1968 he gave a speech to the Conservative Association in Birmingham which the press dubbed 'Rivers of Blood.' In the speech, he criticised immigration to Britain from the Commonwealth and also the government's proposed legislation of Race Relations. Powell said that as he looked ahead, he was "filled with foreboding. Like the Roman, I seem to see 'the River Tiber foaming with much blood'." He was sacked from the Conservative Front Bench by the Conservative leader Edward Heath, for being inflammatory and damaging Race Relations.

Gospel Train
The Gospel Train is a famous spiritual. It was first published in 1872 and became one of the songs of the Fisk Jubilee Singers. Like most spirituals, the words/lyrics have a dual meaning. On the surface it alludes to Christian imagery and meaning, but it is also coded language which slaves used to signal escapes to freedom.

The gospel train is coming
I hear it just at hand
I hear the car wheels moving
And rumbling through the land
Get on board, children (3×)
For there's room for many a more

Grip
A suitcase. Many West Indians had a suitcase packed from the moment they arrived in Britain for their eventual return home.

Holiness Churches
In the early 1900s, a radical form of Protestant Christianity emerged in America as Pentecostals whose central principle is the day of Pentecost, which in the bible is the Jewish festival of weeks. Both Charles Parham (1873-1929) and William James Seymour (1870-1922) (an African American) were the principal people behind this movement. The Azusa Street Revival Meetings in Los Angeles California (1906-1915) started by Seymour, are credited with igniting the worldwide interest in Pentecostalism. Pentecostals emphasise a person's relationship with God through baptism in the holy spirit and the speaking in tongues.

Holy Ghost
Holy Spirit.

Jubilee
Jubilee in the Old Testament in the Bible refers to the ownership and management of land. During this time, in Leviticus, 25:8-13 it states that prisoners should be set free, and people's debts wiped clean. It was a time of freedom and celebration when everyone received back their original property, and slaves were set free.

Lining

'Lining' was a feature of West Indian worship in the early years of being in Britain. The custom was prevalent in America, especially the south and is thought to have begun in Gaelic communities in Scotland. Lining is when a designated person calls out the line of a song before it is sung with the singers responding by singing the line of the song. This process continues until the end of the song.

McCarran-Walter Act 1952

The McCarran-Walter Act, also known as the 1952 Immigration and Nationality Act, limited the flow of West Indian farm workers to the USA. As a result of this restriction, Jamaicans were particularly responsive to Britain's recruitment policy for labourers from the West Indies to go to Britain to work.

Open Air Meeting/Service

These were church services which West Indians held on busy main streets or near to street markets, both as a way of evangelising and also as a way of attracting people to their churches.

Pardner

A pardner is a rotating saving scheme in which family and friends save together which has been popular in Caribbean communities for years.

- Family and friends deposit a fixed amount of money over a fixed period to a person known as the banker who looks after the money as a central fund.
- Each person in the group will take it, in turn, to withdraw all the money from the fund.
- If there are 12 people in a pardner paying £50 over a 12-week period, the banker will pay out £600 each week (12x 50) to a pardner member.

- This process of weekly payments continues until every member of the group has been paid or have received their money draw, (money).

Pastor
The name of a minister or clergy in a Pentecostal church.

Pentecostals
See Holiness Churches

Prayer Meetings
Church services usually held in people's homes during the early years of West Indian Christians' arrival in Britain.

Prelate
Usually a bishop in a church

Pro Tools
Pro Tools is a digital audio workstation which is used for a wide range of sound recording and sound production. It can run as a stand-alone piece of software or with other computerised sound features. It can perform the functions of a multi-track tape recorder and audio mixer.

Publishing Right Society (PRS)
PRS represents songwriters, composer and publishers. It protects its members' performing rights and collects royalties on their behalf whenever their music is played or performed publicly.

Stems
These are the audio mixing materials used in sound recordings before combining them into a final sound mix. Stems are also sometimes referred to as submixes or audio subgroups.

Saints
A general term meaning members or the congregation of a Pentecostal church.

Sound Check
This is the process which performers and sound crew go through before a concert or live performance. It involves making sure that the sound on the stage is to every performer's satisfaction and that the 'front of house' sound is clear, at the right volume and in balance. The person responsible for getting this right is either the performer's or the venue's sound engineer.

Spirituals
Formerly known as 'negro spirituals', the spirituals have their origins in the songs that slaves sang on plantations as they worked. They are mainly Christian songs with themes from the Old Testament. Slaves used to compare their situation to that of the Children of Israel who were in bondage in Egypt and longed to be free. Apart from having Christian messages, many slave songs were coded messages of escape plans.

Swinging Sixties
This was a period of social and cultural change in Britain. It's commonly known as the 'permissive age' because of the young people of that age, relaxed attitude to sex and sexual behaviour. In music, The Beatles and the Mersey Sound were all the rage, and the pill, miniskirt and women's liberation were all significant features of the time.

Technical Rider
A Technical Rider is a document which groups and performers send to a venue, promoter and engineer, which sets out all the technical requirements and stage set up for a band, group or singer's performance. Most Technical Riders set out the PA sound requirements which can range from the simple to the most complex.

Underground Railroad

The Underground Railroad was a network of people and places that offered shelter to escaped slaves from the South. People who helped the slaves on their escape journey were known as 'conductors'. They provided hiding places in private homes, churches and schoolhouses. These were called 'stations', 'safe houses' and 'depots'. The people operating them were called 'stationmasters'. Escaping slaves would walk at night for obvious reasons and when needed 'wade in the water' so that pursuing dogs could not smell their tracks. Spirituals such as *Wade in the Water, The Gospel Train,* and *Swing Low, Sweet Chariot* directly refer to the Underground Railroad.

CPSIA information can be obtained
at www.ICGtesting.com
Printed in the USA
BVHW040945180619
551200BV00037B/1593/P